Imprint

Mary Beth Spray

Beaver's Pond
PRESS

Disclaimer

This is my own personal story of a period in my life as I remember it. I have changed the names of some places and the identities of the characters in order to protect their privacy. Conversations are recreated to evoke the gist of the scene and are not word-for-word transcripts. This is because my autobiographical novel is not about the individuals I described but about my own experience.

ISBN 13: 978-1-64343-581-7
Library of Congress Catalog Number: 2024916674
Printed in the United States of America
First Printing: 2025
29 28 27 26 25   5 4 3 2 1

Book design by Dan Pitts
Editing by Kerry Stapley
Book typeset in Minion Pro

BEAVER'S POND PRESS

Beaver's Pond Press
939 Seventh Street West
Saint Paul, MN 55102
(952) 829-8818
www.BeaversPondPress.com

Visit the author's website at marybethspray.com

"Who would deduce the dragonfly from the larva,
the iris from the bud, the lawyer from the infant? . . .
We are all shape-shifters and magical reinventors.
Life is really a plural noun, a caravan of selves."

—Diane Ackerman

To my husband Dave, for his patient and loving support.

Chapter 1

It was June 1984—I stepped off the plane onto the boarding stairs in Pierre, South Dakota, and felt the familiar blast of dry heat. Elm and cottonwood trees bubbled over the small river town. As far as my eyes could see, dark clouds formed a visible storm still thirty miles away. The state capitol building stood out like a middle finger on the Missouri River bluff. Trauma from my childhood and marriage originated here. My body felt connected to this murky town. It was part of my DNA; it was *imprinted* on me. That day, I did what I had always done with trauma. Stuffed it.

I was thirty-four, a mother of three children. For the last ten months, my husband Ken and I had lived in our new home in Barrington, Rhode Island. It was a dream come true, and I couldn't wait to share the East Coast wonders with my Pierre friends and family. I packed pictures to show them how close I was to Narragansett Bay and so they could see the stunning colonial home I had chosen. I couldn't wait to brag about being the professor's wife on the East Coast, the Limón dance classes I took at Brown, and the new friends I had made. All that joy covered up the dark marriage of the last twelve years that I tried to salvage. I was relieved to get away from Ken and decided to cherish that week by getting reacquainted with the ministry leaders I loved and by hanging out with my family. He paid for the plane ticket and called my dad to make the arrangements to pick me up. He said with a smile that I should greet everyone for him. I couldn't believe the good fortune of me being the first of us to return to Pierre. He usually was the one to be first.

I settled in the front seat that used to be Mom's. Outside the passenger window, I noticed the familiar, dilapidated homes of the Indigenous community. South Dakota houses the poorest reservation in the US, the Pine Ridge Reservation. Doors were off their hinges, and broken chairs were strewn around the grassless yards. Then emerged the elegant homes near the Missouri River bottom.

"I love that all three of you came to pick me up at the airport. Don't you all have to work today?" I cranked my neck to glance back at my brother and sister's faces.

"Looks like you lost weight, Mary Beth," my look-alike sister Susan said as she scratched her scalp through her hair-sprayed pouf.

"Thanks!" I didn't mention that my stomach had been in knots. I could barely eat. In Barrington, Ken had made jealous accusations that my friendship with a student went too far.

"How was the flight?" Dad asked.

I turned to him in the soft leather seat that cradled me like a baby. "Good!" Out past Dad, a yellow sunflower field brought up past nightmares about a period of my life when I was in a daze and couldn't control my body's actions. The view gave me a gut ache.

"I'm excited to see everyone! How's Pam, Ross? I want to spend some time with my sister-in-law this week." I smiled back at him.

With a blank face and no eye contact, he said, "Well, Mary Beth, we're taking you straight to the alcoholic treatment center." His voice was monotone. "Ken called us, and we decided that you should get some help."

"What! Me? But I don't drink! Who decided that?" Now the nightmares exploded as if I'd stepped on a landmine and blown those sunflowers to pieces. I leaned on the car-door panel and glowered. The rearview mirror reflected the sunflowers that seemed to be staring at me in shame as we passed. My heart pounded and tears welled. I shook my head with a furrowed brow and scrutinized them, looking for an explanation. He'd set up this whole trip as a pretense. He had hoodwinked my family. They believed I was an alcoholic.

Ross's patronizing smile said it all. "Well, you're just going to answer questions, and the treatment counselors will decide if you should stay or not. But as of now, you'll be staying there this week."

"Ross!" I pleaded. "Ken told me I was coming for a vacation, and I was planning on visiting the youth leaders and you all!" I felt lightheaded. "Dad?"

His handsome face with white sideburns turned away from me. "This is an intervention, Mary Beth."

"But Dad, I don't understand! Who decided this? Ken?"

Ross gazed out the window without answering. We passed streets of light-colored ramblers in the predictable muteness of households that mask pain.

"They can't keep me, I'm not an alcoholic," was the only defiance I could muster as I laid my head back and closed my eyes. For a moment, I saw myself thirteen years ago on the Paris Métro, gazing out the window at the passing bistros. How wonderful it had felt to have a day to take my journal and sit with my feet up on the concrete ledge at the fountains of the Luxembourg Gardens. Without fighting back, my insides caved, wondering if Ken could somehow make me a prisoner. He had sent me there to my dad to get straightened out like I was a kid to be reprimanded. Pierre was where trauma held me captive, where people believed a minister, and where men had power over women. I wondered if this was how he was going to keep me from her.

Madonna's song "Like a Virgin" played on KCCR. The words "Didn't know how lost I was until I found you" reminded me of Melo. She was Ken's student, and I loved her. She lifted my spirits and supported me as I had never experienced before. I stopped shuddering recalling her kisses all over my body at the monastery.

Questions roiled in my head, and the trace of stale cigarettes in Dad's Lincoln made me sick. *They must have talked long distance, and somehow Ken convinced them that I needed incarceration. He knows I don't drink. What power does he feel he needs to wield? What is he afraid of? He persuaded my family to do his dirty work while he sat in Rhode Island. He conned me, his own wife, into taking a vacation to Pierre to visit family and friends whom I hadn't seen for a year. It took cold, calculated thinking. Was this a kidnapping or a mastermind move to scare me? How many phone calls did he make? He pinpointed my dad, thinking he'd still have authority over me. Did he think I might bolt and decide he needed the muscle of my brother's presence?*

Both Ken's dad and my dad drank, and our families were scarred by alcoholism. Ken's dad chased his mom with a knife—always jealous. My dad hid his drinking and pill-taking, so my angry mom became the visible problem. Two family divorces over alcohol between Ken and me.

I'd heard stories that as a student at the University of South Dakota, Ken drank to the point of falling asleep at the wheel in an intersection. He also took speed before tests. His family laughed at stories of him standing drunk on a coffee table. I didn't drink in college, not even in France! And I still don't.

Dad, Susan, and Ross were all recovering alcoholics. As far as I knew, they weren't drinking now. My three family members must have believed whatever Ken told them. His influence over the individuals he groomed was creepy. Ken was charismatic. We'd been married twelve years, and in that time, he'd developed a formidable sway over my relatives in Pierre. I wondered if, as alcoholics themselves, they were easier to convince. Were my mom and other sister, Lucy, contacted? They would have protested and ripped him a new asshole. They wanted nothing to do with Ken and his manipulations.

We crossed the Missouri River and pulled up to a small brick hospital I had visited six years before for my dad's family week. This hospital had been a place of happy memories, the place where my family had come clean and shared our feelings with my dad and each other during his healing from alcoholism. This was where we all experienced honesty for the first time in our family. Back then, when I made eye contact with my father's blue eyes, the air had cleared. Now it was something else entirely.

I quickly composed myself before getting out of the car. I took a deep breath, counted to ten, and lifted my chin. *Oh Jesus, protect me from the man I married!*

"I'll take your suitcase," Ross said, reaching for the suitcase handle.

"I can do it." I took a step backward and jerked my suitcase behind me. A hot flush rushed through my face. "What? You think I have pills and drugs in here? You're ganging up on me! All of you!" I screamed.

"No," Ross said, "we're supposed to handle your things. They're going to go through them in the treatment center."

My whole body was shaking. Dad was having an affair, Ross worked with Ken in the ministry, and Susan was on a second marriage. Who were they to judge me based on hearsay? My loyal family treated me like a criminal. Thoughts of Melo popped in and out of my mind. I wanted her arms around me and her voice saying everything would be all right.

The hot wind was stronger on the platform. We walked up the granite stairs without a word, my purse strap over my shoulder. Dad led the climb while Ross waited for me to follow. Dad carried my suitcase. Susan trailed behind us.

"Welcome to our treatment center." A smiling man in a dark suit held out his hand to Dad. "And hello, Francis. Good to see you again." He turned to me. "Hello, Mary Beth. I'm Dr. Larson. Come with me to the nurse's office, and we'll do intake." He knew my name already. He was expecting us. "Thank you, Francis, we'll take it from here."

I tried to keep my tears inside by swallowing several times. Dad's blue eyes were averted, as were Ross's. Susan's tight lips were pointed downward. My sweet dad who'd occasionally given me five dollars and taken me to lunch. My sister Lucy had gotten one hundred dollars every once in a while, because she knew more about Dad's affair. Ross was closest in age to me. He used to tell me which boys had approached him and wanted to meet me. Susan was quiet and forgotten because she was noiseless. How much had Ken shared with them? Why hadn't they contacted me first and asked me what was going on? The anger buried inside me tightened my jaw. They knew I didn't drink. I felt hijacked. This was more than an intervention. It was an abduction! And my errant husband was a minister, no less. The only reason he could have concocted this travesty was my relationship with his student Melo. I hadn't yet admitted to him that my connection with her was anything more than friendship. I denied it to him. No doubt Ken was mortified. But this revenge was pure evil and hardly spiritual. How could I explain this to the doctor? He must have concocted a story around my drinking after telling everyone that I was having a lesbian affair.

"Wait for me," I said, trying to sound confident to Dad, Ross, and Susan. "I won't be long."

I searched for answers in their faces, but they turned away. I couldn't look at them any longer. I was ashamed of them.

Maybe I just walk out and cross the Missouri River Bridge on foot, I thought. *Hitchhiking like I did before I was married, fourteen years ago. Would they hold me by force?*

I had no money in my pocket. I was totally at their disposal. Women weren't believed in the religious scheme of things then. And Ken, the one I had proclaimed my love to in front of a congregation at St. Peter and Paul Catholic Church, orchestrated it all and pulled the strings.

The nurses' station looked like an old-fashioned counter with a well-lit open-framed window. A picture of the canyons of South Dakota's Badlands hung on the wall. A lone buffalo grazed, abandoned and insignificant.

Why am I here? By now, I should be visiting old friends, having a hamburger at the Woodhouse Restaurant, I remember thinking.

Dr. Larson interrupted my thoughts. I took him to be in his early forties. His black hair was beginning to gray. He looked sturdy in his black suit coat. His voice was soft, but his dark eyes looked hard and forbidding. "The nurse is going to go through your suitcase and look for alcohol, drugs, and pills."

"Here." I unlatched the suitcase, defiant and perplexed. I wanted to dump it on the floor, thrust my bathing suit in his face, scream that I'd packed for a vacation, not to become strung out and wasted. But instead, I obeyed. They wouldn't find anything.

"No, we'll do it. Sit down. Would you like a cup of coffee?" The coffee smelled good, camouflaging the intake office's antiseptic odor. I tried to pray, but I couldn't find the words inside me.

They took the open suitcase I had eagerly packed that morning, set it up on a counter, and exposed the contents. Out came my folded best blue jeans; sandals; T-shirts for a week; a copy of *The Clan of the Cave Bear*; Oil of Olay; raggedy underwear; worn-out, stretchy bras; and a swimsuit. My personals for a week were displayed on the counter, fingered by these strangers. They opened an envelope and pulled out my photos of the newly purchased colonial Rhode Island home and a few shots of the ocean.

The doctor left my things, ushered me into a gloomy room, and sat across from me in a leather chair. "Tell us about your drinking."

"I don't drink. I shouldn't be here."

"Well, let us decide that."

"Is this about last week?" I assumed Ken had talked to them.

"What happened last week?"

"My husband and I were yelling, actually screaming, at each other. That day, after we gave each other the silent treatment, I asked for two of those twist-off sugar drinks that have alcohol in them. A daiquiri and a mai tai."

"What were you arguing about?"

I made a face. Then I gave him the truth. "I was involved with a woman."

Dr. Larson ignored this bitter admission and adjusted his black-rimmed glasses. "What else have you drunk in this last year?"

"Well, nothing else really this year, but the year before I had a glass of wine at Thanksgiving, one at Christmas, and one at our Easter family gathering."

He rose and left the intake room. I looked around the room, still not believing I was there. I gripped the arms of the chair. Afraid to move, I wondered who was going to pay for this. Probably Dad. Ken siphoned money off anyone. He had plenty of donors. And he was not afraid to ask. *What a weasel!*

The doctor's phone was sitting on his desk. I desperately wanted to call Melo. *Oh, Melo, what would you do in this situation?* Melo had given me a taste of freedom. She wouldn't tolerate even the slightest control. She would walk out and find a way back to Rhode Island, end of story.

But I was not her. My thoughts went to the first time I met her.

I opened the front door.

"Hi, I'm Melo Claire. I'm here for mentoring," the young college-aged woman announced with an easy voice. She stepped over the threshold into the entryway, examining my home's interior. I stood aside so she would notice the splendid white staircase that was a midpoint in the symmetry of my colonial home in Barrington.

I fit the role of minister's wife perfectly by spending time with wives of committee folks and with the female leaders and girls. At the college level, we called it mentoring even though I had no formal training in mentoring.

Her thin, mousy-colored bangs stuck to her forehead. The rest of her hair was straight and shoulder length. Slim and athletic, she brought in a whiff of the dried autumn leaves while fiddling with the wire rings of a notebook.

"Hey, Melo, I'm excited to get to know you. Ken mentioned to me that you're talented—especially with dancing on desks!" I teased as my arm gestured toward the living room. Part of the strategy of winning followers in the ministry was to use humor.

"Nice room," she said in a monotone voice. She perched upright on the couch and twiddled the collar on her blue-and-red-striped polo shirt, her Bible in her lap. Her eyes settled for a second on my Degas print of dancers tying their toe shoes. "I saw you at the auditorium for our convocation. I liked how

you did a ballet bow with your hands out to the side holding a pretend long dress when Ken introduced you." Smiling finally, she looked at me directly with radiant blue eyes shrouded in straight, long lashes.

A twinge of intrigue flushed through me as I cleared my throat. I was delighted she had noticed me. "But you're not a very good actor in skits," she said.

Blushing, I kicked my shoes off and slid my legs over the arm of the chair. "Your Beverly Bunny skit was hilarious. You are *a good actor," I countered. I already liked her.*

"And Ken is a rather good teacher," she said. "I love what he's saying in class. Today he said how God chose each one of us and that we're called to befriend kids. He makes me feel special. I can't wait to hear more of his ideas about ministry and feeling important." Her lips stayed parted, exposing a white patch on her front tooth.

"Do you feel the same as him?" she asked.

"Pretty much. His words made me feel special when I first met him." I was proud that she revered my husband—most people did gravitate toward him. "We feel called upon to be here. We offer our lives to you, Melo. We're about healing." I echoed Ken's rhetoric as best I could. But I didn't want to sound preachy. How refreshing it was to have this young woman in front of me. She reminded me of the freedom I didn't have.

It was her eyes—piercing and holding mine—that hooked me.

"Well, I need healing." She looked down. Her long, strong nose resembled Sean Penn's. "I just want to be happy and have a purpose like you and Ken seem to."

We were far from happy. Ken and I had a dark history in Pierre and subsequently here in Barrington. And I had to do mental backflips to make his violence and my belief and worship of him seem normal in my head. But I just smiled, took her hand, and promised her the world.

The coffee in the treatment center tasted stale. I let the white Styrofoam cup sit on the table. I heard Dr. Larson talking on the phone in the next room to Susan, Dad, and Ross to verify that what I had said was true. He called Ken too. I heard laughing.

Ken had captivated me when I first met him. I saw his hazel eyes looking at me from afar while he was talking to my friends in the cool church basement. He had a way of remembering names. He remembered mine from when my friend Debra and I were leading the singing at contemporary Mass with his brother Joe on the guitar. He laughed often and looked like Robert Redford. My friends surrounded him. When he spoke, I melted inside. His deep voice was smooth, especially when he talked of Jesus as a friend.

A bell went off behind the nurse, and the phone rang. Dr. Larson came back into his office where I was sitting. Although the South Dakota sun warmed the dim room, I still shivered. He shut the door and stood behind his desk.

"We found no proof of you being an alcoholic." His voice was unreasonably loud. He pulled out a letter and waved it above his head; it was my handwriting. He leaned forward and hit the letter on his desk with every word. "But. What. Is. This?"

I blinked.

"If my wife wrote a letter like this to another woman, I would divorce her. Why don't you get a divorce?"

"Divorce is not an option," I recycled my mantra.

Back in the reception room, I picked up the phone receiver and called Dad even though I had asked him to stay and wait. The nurse stood and watched me. I lugged my suitcase to the top step and searched through my disheveled purse for a tissue. The austere streets repulsed me compared to the kelp-scented shores of Rhode Island. In the dry heat, I rubbed my eyes. I waited for Dad on the cement step. In my heart, I stood naked on that horrific pedestal for all to see.

My brother, groomed by Ken, was now a local leader in Ken's same youth ministry. Ross developed leaders where he lived. Dad admired Ken's ability to surround himself with important men in the city like wealthy businessmen and governors. For a while, Ken was on the state pardon board. I was my dad's firstborn child, his daughter, and yet, absent were questions about how Ken treated me. Dad lived with his longtime girlfriend; Mom had moved to St. Paul, Minnesota. My Pierre family rejected me, and Rhode Island was over a thousand miles away. I suddenly missed my mom, her direct questions, her dislike for Ken—she'd held her tongue early on, but then admitted her loathing of him once I declared my decision to marry him.

I inhaled as Dad drove up. He didn't get out, so I put my suitcase in the back seat and got in the front. He didn't say much. A conservative news show was on the radio. We crossed over River Road, where I used to drive Mom's red convertible to a summer school typing class, blaring Buffalo Springfield's "For What It's Worth." I used to take the long way along the river to let off steam and get out of the house longer.

I did recognize that they thought they were doing their duty, and that Ken had orchestrated this visit to scare me. Ken knew that I would not divorce him and that my mindset was still governed by the evangelical position of submission to the husband.

I wanted to refrain from explaining to Dad (and now everyone in Pierre) how I loved Melo and what boundaries we had crossed. It didn't feel safe because I felt shame.

I called Melo right away from my dad's condominium. She was appalled and wanted to come to Pierre, but I nixed it.

My family members believed what Ken said. The prior week, I had been in my Barrington, Rhode Island, home, where we had been living for nine months. Next thing I knew, Ken and the kids were traveling in the camper van from the East Coast to Pierre, South Dakota. I'd been instructed to drive Dad's car to a KOA campground in Minnesota to meet them. The night before I left, I had a dream that I was driving a huge bus and could not get my foot on the brake pedal. The bus went out of control, crashing into a river. It went down in the water. Kept going down, down.

Chapter 2

Within a week, my children and Ken reached the Minnesota KOA campground in our VW camper van. Their grim faces lit up as soon as I opened my arms and knelt before them. I picked up my toddler, Paul, and kissed his cheek with a loud screech. Six-year-old Chris ran past me, and I caught him by the chest for a hug. Gabrielle's eyes searched mine as I embraced her and whispered in her ear, "How have you been doing, sweetheart?"

Motherhood was a time of self-love for me. I knew my role, and my life had a purpose. I was the most important person in my children's lives, especially in their early years. I had power, made decisions for them, and defended those choices fiercely. I purposely made memories for each of them. Gabrielle, my firstborn, planted tomato seedlings with me that I had harvested from under a grow light. I signed her up for painting classes, which I had also enjoyed as a kid. When Chris was born, I saw signs of stress in Gabrielle. She pulled out hairs around her forehead. One time I heard a slap followed by the baby crying. I rushed to where Gabrielle was standing. I had just learned about sharing feelings at my dad's family week. I ran to the sound of the baby wailing and knelt at eye level with Gabrielle in front of the baby. "Gabrielle, sweetheart, how do you feel when you make your brother cry like that?"

She said, "I feel better!"

I picked up the baby and pulled her aside eye to eye. "Gabrielle, he needs a strong and smart big sister to sing a song. Could you sing 'This Little Light of Mine' to him?" She looked at him. Her stubby pointer finger went straight up and bounced to her singing until baby Chris smiled.

Motherhood was a time when I could insert my ideas and beliefs into my children. I was in control, directing them to have everything: good health, self-confidence, feelings, and artistic expression. I wanted them to love life and go for their dreams.

A group of young mothers and I met at the end of a semitruck, and we divided up blocks of cheeses, carob, and lecithin in a kind of early co-op. I used the book *More-with-Less Cookbook* to make granola and meals. I needed to use my grocery allotment from Ken wisely, and I wanted the healthiest food for my children. Chris loved my homemade yogurt and smiled all the time with his fat cheeks. Cooking became my outlet to try new things.

Paul, our youngest, was cared for by his big brother and sister. They loved seeing him getting a bath in the bassinet. They both wanted to help with the new baby. I poured a pitcher of warm water into a pliable plastic container. Then I unwrapped Paul, talking to him in a baby-talk voice, took his cloth diaper off, and lowered him into the warm water.

"He likes it!" Chris squealed and clapped. We quickly rubbed no-tears baby soap and water all over Paul, especially on his bottom. They laughed when I turned him over to expose his butt, and his arms and legs started jumping.

"Gabrielle, could you get me the baby towel from underneath the bassinet?"

Three children changed my life enormously. I took Paul on my hip everywhere.

At the campground, I wouldn't look at Ken. I wanted to scream at him and tear his eyes out, but he held the keys to Barrington. He came toward me with his arms open. I turned and snubbed him. "Kids! Who wants to help me make mac and cheese?"

"I will!" Chris jumped in the air with his arm up.

"Let's all do it together in the camper."

Ken and I had bought this lime-green camper in hopes of fun travel and camping. It was self-sufficient. Gabrielle slept over the front seat in a hammock. The top popped up so we could stand while cooking, and then it transformed into another bed. The table doubled into a bed along with seats that bent down. Ken stuck his head in with a smile to say he was making the fire and reading the Bible. I didn't respond.

"Daddy, come make mac and cheese with us!"

He looked at me for a few seconds with his handsome eyes—a reminder of the love I once felt for him.

"No, looks too crowded to me. I'm making the fire for the wieners."

"OK! Isn't this fun, Mommy?"

"Yes. I missed you last week. What did you eat with Daddy?"

"Pizza!" Then Chris looked up at me. "Why are we going to visit Grandpa? I miss Rhode Island. I want to go back to my friends," he said.

"I miss Rhode Island too. We'll return in a couple of weeks." I bit on my fingernail and spat it out.

Chris stared at me and yelled, "Melo loves mac and cheese," his hairline wet with playful sweat.

The lump in my throat at the sound of her name made it hard for me to swallow.

I glanced at Ken through the window as he read by the fire. An otter glided silently on the Crow River without seeming to notice us. Dusk set in. As I gazed out the open window from inside the camper, a bat swirled before me. I stood motionless, unafraid of the bat. Rather, I felt a connection. Both of us were outliers in a holiday land of campers. In the window, my reflection revealed my sunken cheeks. I traced my hips and cupped my breasts. Everything felt smaller. My once-bulging calves were now just slightly curved. I ran my fingers through my hair and wondered when it had grown out so long and stringy.

An American redstart's high-pitched chirp and downward inflection interrupted my thoughts. Her dull-brown color and flicker of yellow flashed before me, and I could only hear her, the crickets, and trucks passing on the nearby highway.

Chris was my eater, mostly because he was so active. Paul sang along with the radio: "Might as well face it, you're ditted to love." His beautiful mass of light-brown curls bounced as he jumped to the music.

Chris grabbed Paul's stuffed bunny and danced it in the air. "Hey Paul, guess what? I'm ditted to love, dumb head."

"Gabrielle, will you get the buns from Daddy?"

"Should I set the table in here, Mom?"

"Actually, let's eat outside on the picnic table." I didn't want to squeeze in next to Ken.

Gabrielle, my talkative ten-year-old girl who'd been unusually quiet that night, came to my rescue. "Chris. Leave Paul alone."

I gathered her pigtails in my hand and stroked her hair. "Thank you, sweetie."

We brought the saucepan of packaged mac and cheese to the picnic table. Ken wanted to say a prayer and hold hands. I held Paul on my hip and ignored his outstretched hand.

"Dear Lord, thank you for this food and all the many hands who made it." He looked at all of us with a smile until we opened our eyes. "And thank you for bringing Mommy back to us. Amen." Then he clapped to encourage the kids to clap. Ken was jovial.

Paul sat in my lap while he ate the pieces of hot dog I cut up. I couldn't eat. I did the dishes while Ken put the kids to bed.

The phone booth I'd seen earlier made me think of Melo. I had to call her. I gathered my toiletries. "I'm going to shower." As I walked down the dirt road through the maze of RVs, I focused on the well-lit pole that peeked through the trees, guiding me toward the entrance of the campground. I emerged from a copse of birch trees and stepped into the phone booth's glow. I called Melo collect.

"It's me!" I said, my words no longer heavy.

"Oh, Mare, I've been worried! It's you! I'm lonely for you. I can't even stand to be around anyone."

A tickle twirled deep in my groin. "I'm so sorry you're sad. I'm not doing too well, either. My life has turned upside down. Can you believe I'm in a Minnesota campground since I talked to you last week on the phone in Pierre? I miss you."

"When are you coming back to Barrington? Your house is quiet."

"I know. Ken drove out here from Rhode Island with the kids. It looks like we're going to stay in Pierre for a few weeks. He instructed me to meet him and the kids here in Minnesota. My hopes and dreams are disappearing."

"Oh, Mare, I'm so sorry. I'm coming!"

"No, I'll figure it out."

I pushed the phone close to my ear. I wanted to hear her breathe; then she whispered, "Are you looking at the stars?"

The lamplight blinded my eyes.

"Just like that yellow star will never fall from the sky, I will never leave you. Mare, I'm here."

I was afraid to consider what she believed.

"Mare. Everything will be all right. God will take care of us. Can you feel me kissing you? I'm hugging you. You are my heart."

A shadow darkened the road. When the figure reached the light, I could see it was Ken charging toward me, his blond hair sticking out sideways. I dropped the phone and let it dangle from its cord as his slitted eyes thrust into my face. "This shit has got to stop!"

My rigid frame pressed against the glass. Melo's soothing voice at the end of the cord dangled in the protective booth.

Mustard breath blared at me.

"What the frit are you doing?" He slammed the phone down. Campers started to emerge from tents and RVs. "You are going to pay for this, Mary Beth." He wrenched a handful of hair at the nape of my neck and dragged me out of the booth into the middle of the campground entrance.

I tumbled backward, landing on my butt, scraping my elbows. He stood over me as I tried to get up, but I had no leverage. With my feet flat on the russet gravel, I found footing, but he shoved me, and my tailbone pummeled into the gravel. Above me, I could see the KOA sign. His feet stomped the ground and his voice echoed. "This is the last time you will ever speak to her. Do you understand me?"

White dust was all over my shoes and shorts. I sat on the ground and pulled my knees close to my chest. My elbows burned. A large man from the crowd stepped closer and crossed his arms. A woman stood next to the stranger with her hands on her hips. One other couple glanced sideways at us before her husband led her away.

"Get up," Ken said. I obeyed. He grabbed me by the arm and dragged me down the road. With a handful of hair, he pulled my head back. Seeing my bewilderment, he sputtered, "I knew you were up to something. So eager to shower."

My nail-bitten fingers combed through my hair. "Stop. People are watching. You left the kids alone. Let's just go back to the van."

"Never do that again!" he said, poking his finger into my chest. "There is no room for Melo in our lives, Mary Beth! None," he said with finality.

"Melo loves our family!" I shouted.

15

"You'll get used to it. End of story. No more Melo!" He turned and investigated the crowd that was still growing, then walked back.

Disoriented and afraid, I proceeded in the direction of our camper but lost my way; my tears flowed. I feared he'd come back if I did not move fast enough. Finally, a small light peeked through the camper curtains. *Lord Jesus, bring my family safely back to Rhode Island. Restore the hope I first had when we moved there a year ago.*

I looked to the sky. Orion winked into the darkness. The nape of my neck burned. I shook.

Our children slept. The trees were still and breezeless. I grabbed a jacket. I had to pee and refused to use the porta-potty under Ken's surveillance. I avoided the phone booth and took a circuitous route.

He did not follow me or say anything when I returned. I retreated to my submissive state.

Lying in bed in the camper, he asked, "Did you touch her, ever?"

I thought about lying, but said, "Yes, once on the breast."

"Did you touch her anywhere else?"

I thought of her lips on my skin and her breath in my ear. Our faces cheek to cheek. I said, in a tiny voice, "No."

The night camping sounds settled in. I wasn't sure I could cope, living day to day with Ken. My heart was icy when I thought of him. The next morning, we broke down camp and headed for Pierre, where we had lived for over thirty years, and where people worshipped him.

Chapter 3

One year earlier in Barrington at an East Coast college in 1983, Ken's initiation into the academic world clicked. Every day he came home with stories I relished. He had become the favorite son of Pierre, South Dakota, and I anticipated the same success for him in Barrington, Rhode Island. I relied on his keen skill of drawing remarkable people to him, people who impressed me. For the first time in a while, I forgot the trials of our eleven years of marriage and was optimistic. I felt dignified being married to a college teacher, especially on the East Coast, far from the Midwest. I had attained my dream of being admired and respected.

Ever since I heard the lion roar of the waves when I visited California at the age of eighteen, I wanted that energy in my life. I had craved a life by the sea since then. I could see the edge of the planet when I looked out from shore. I could breathe larger. I could smell freedom. The movement of the waves tugged at my kinesthetic spirit. The ocean gave me an upsurge of feeling that the Creator was near to my soul.

A year previous, I had coaxed Ken to think about another career and to live by the ocean. "I'm thinking we should try something new, Ken. What about a job on the East Coast? Maybe teaching, something different from youth ministry?" I said as I wiped off the white countertop.

"Yeah, I think I've reached a plateau here with youth ministry. I'll pray about it." He brought over the dinner dishes from the dining table and embraced me. Ken had contacts all over the country from his ministry. "What about your ballet studio?" His hand caressed my shoulder.

"Oh, I could teach wherever we go!" I said with a smile, doing a pirouette.

He wanted to make me happy, and he did when he agreed to pursue teaching positions, a momentous change from eleven years of youth ministry. Together we said *yes* to a move across the country to Rhode Island. I felt lucky because he considered my dreams and opinions in his decision. We settled in the two-story dream house of my choosing, five minutes from the ocean.

At that time, I believed that only he could make this dream of mine happen. I held onto a belief from before we were married, one that said that Ken, the man, would make all my dreams come true. Right off the bat, he arranged for us to honeymoon in Colorado Springs while he went to classes at a youth ministry master's program. We house-sat in a modern circular house on the side of a mountain. We entertained at the round house; I made crêpes for the professors and staff. I adored all the things Ken could do in his classes, the way he challenged his teachers and engaged with them, joking and treating them as peers. We made friends with the other leaders and their wives. I took a class on the art of presentations and received praises for my movement-based performance. A teacher whose political views were different than ours became a friend to me. Watergate was all the news. It was exciting to meet folks from all over the United States and to rub shoulders with the professors. We came back to Colorado Springs two years later when Nixon was resigning. I took dance classes with Hanya Holm, a noted modern dancer. Ken talked about his contacts all over the United States and said we would be visiting them. He not only introduced me to God in a personal way; he also took me to unseen places. He spoke enthusiastically and gave me hope in the times when women could only marry, have kids, and be a secretary, teacher, or nurse. Women's desires were manifested through the men they married, or at least that's what I thought. And I had married the "rock star" of Pierre. Everyone respected him. I admired how he used popular music of the time, like the *Jesus Christ Superstar* album, to entice younger folks to the church. I melted at the sound of the Mary Magdalene character singing, "I don't know how to love him." Ken used the *Tommy* album to entice other followers.

He chose me as his wife, and I was happy to be at his side taking in all the accolades of his charisma. This was the man who broke rules—rules of the Catholic church—rules I struggled with.

After we were married, we got involved with the charismatic movement and "the gifts of the Holy Spirit." We spoke in tongues as another form of praying. Ken said he had the gift of discernment. A man with the gift of healing came to our home. When someone complained of a back problem, he prayed over their legs and one grew to the same length as the other, curing the back problem. I was not completely convinced that a leg could grow, but these prayer times filled me with awe and made me feel important. We watched Oral Roberts's show on TV and sent money to his church. If I had any objection to what the Pentecostal movement proclaimed, I kept quiet. Many people thought it was bullshit. I'd had the same feeling about my parents' involvement in the John Birch Society when I was young; it was a feeling of being weird because I believed these outlandish theories that many thought were conspiratorial and cultish.

Now we had landed in Rhode Island, and my new stately home and the whiff of the ocean were a dream come true. When I heard from Ken how the college students admired him, I felt honored, because when someone liked my husband, I was liked too. My persona melted into Ken's. I tried to be like him and to read the books he read. He shared his love for the author C. S. Lewis. He loved Henri Nouwen's writings on mysticism. At Ken's suggestion, I devoured *Man's Search for Meaning* by Viktor Frankl. I was inspired by learning of how everything can be taken from us except the freedom and attitude to choose our own way. Ken read the *Autobiography of Malcolm X*. When I didn't have time to read it all, he studied, and I relied on his reading for me and speaking for me. He pored over the Bible along with Bible commentaries for hours in the early morning. I admired his thirst for knowledge. I had a low self-image and no sense of agency.

As the official youth ministry major teacher at the Christian college in Rhode Island, he arranged for me to mentor some of his female students every week just as I had done in Pierre.

Ken directed Melo to me, describing her as one of the "key" female leaders. In his former youth ministry, the leaders targeted "key" kids. These were young folks who could bring more kids to the meetings because they were popular in some way. He relayed how Melo asked tons of questions, volunteered to be a leader, and stayed after class to tell jokes. Our weekly meetings consisted of her talking about her life and school, and me listening. We shared our spiritual lives. I found out about her love of sports and told her I would attend a few of her sports events. I told her about my desire to teach French, and that teaching ballet was an alternative. I had taught ballet in a campus building for a few months. The Christian cocoon kept me sequestered from the world.

I tried to encourage subjects we had in common like music and dancing. She thought I resembled Pat Benatar, one of her favorite singers. She also added that she and her roommate Megan fought a lot.

But she didn't know that I also lived with someone with a penchant for arguments, violence, and control. He would get out his Day-Timer calendar booklet. "OK, Mary Beth, let's set up our dates to make love for the next few weeks. What about Monday and Thursday this week?" He looked at me with a pen in hand and the Day-Timer in the other. "No, wait, I have a meeting until late on Thursday. How about . . ." He rubbed his forehead with his hand and turned the page. "Saturday!" He gave a big laugh.

I was exhausted every night by nine. "Well, I guess, that's OK, if it's right after I put the kids to bed."

"I just got done with lacrosse. Sorry, I'm late," Melo said as she came in the front door.

My chest filled with emotion because of my anticipation at seeing her again. I remember the outdoor smell as I scanned her knee socks and skort. She sat on the toy box to take off her cleats.

"I don't want to mess up your rug with these." She lowered them with two fingers onto the doormat.

I led her to the living room. As we talked about lacrosse, I had a big desire to stand on the sidelines and watch her run and maneuver the ball. I also wanted to play any sport other than cheerleading. Title IX had become law only after I graduated from college. I mentioned jogging with other teachers' wives to look hip and athletic in Melo's eyes.

She picked up Chris's *Star Wars* spaceship and found a button that lit it up. We waited in silence for a second.

I took a breath. "You think we're perfect, but Ken and I fight too. We are hoping to change now that we are out of Pierre. We are both seeing a nun at a monastery, Sister Margaret. We pray together." I looked at her. She held my eyes, not shying away from this new truth that I, too, needed mentoring and prayer. "My prayer time is vital to my serenity, Melo. For the first few minutes, I give thanks for what I have. Eventually, I write my current worries in my notebook, and I let them go, which adds to my inner peace. Ken and I pray together often, if not daily. Would you like to pray with me?"

"Yes." She bowed her head.

"Thank you, Jesus, for this new friendship between Melo and me. Keep us safe and draw us into a trusting and caring relationship. And just like my relationship with you will never be broken, keep Melo and me in your care." My voice trembled. I swallowed and told my body to quiet down. *"Amen."*

Chapter 4

I set the stage with homemade chocolate-chip cookies and a pot of chamomile tea. The handmade quilted tea cozy held the aroma. One sip of the steamy brew calmed my breathing. I rested my head on the back of the flowered chair. I wanted to impress Melo with an organized home and send her back to the dorm feeling supported by me.

"You're going to love those cookies," I promised.

"Oh, am I?" Finally cracking a smile, she took a handful of cookies from a plate. "What a clean house. Where are the toys and the kids?"

"They're hiding," I teased, feeling playful.

After a few sips and bites of cookie, she started talking in a monotone voice, as if she had said it all before. She had been molested by a neighbor man at a young age. *Molested,* I thought, *what exactly does that mean?* But I did not ask. As a silent listener, not a trained counselor, I was hesitant about what to say next. Her honesty around pain struck me. She was a genuine young woman who was looking for spiritual truth.

We met every Tuesday that fall and into the winter. She turned twenty that December. Melo dropped by, sometimes unannounced, mostly to see the kids after school. She kept candy in her pockets, something we didn't have around the house. She would engage the kids with games and wrestling while I baked caramel rolls. Her silly jokes lured them to her. They liked it when I laughed at Melo.

But our actual connection came when we prayed together and shared our deepest feelings in a prayer poem. Prayer notes are prayer with a pen and paper. They're a way to touch a person without touching. This evolved because I wanted her to know that I was thinking of her and praying. Her thoughts written in a poem on a folded note inspired me:

> My heart swells with love watching you mother your children.
> You are a dancing mother, a fun mother, a loving mother.
> When I look at the stars at night, I am overwhelmed by the power of God in our lives.
> *She* will take care of us and keep us close.

When Melo went to visit her brother, I immediately sat down and wrote a letter to her about missing our Tuesday time.

> I will miss you, Melo, when you are gone.
> I will miss your energy and your eyes holding mine.
> Your smiles.
> Your crazy jokes.
> Mostly I will miss you.
> My heart fills with joy when I think of you.

Ken noticed and asked with a frown what I was writing. That was the first time I realized Ken might not appreciate the excitement I experienced with this new relationship in my heart.

Melo invited me to her basketball game. I did not have time to go but showed up another evening when Ken had time to babysit while my goulash casserole baked. It was thrilling for me to witness her movements on the court. When she looked up at me in the bleachers, I felt a twinge and sent a smile back. I felt young again. When she made a basket, I stood and yelled. I never played competitive sports. I had only cheered for them. Attending events was acceptable to Ken; it was part of his ministry style to meet the student where she played, hang out, and earn her friendship on her turf.

When I returned from the game, the hamburger hot dish filled the house with a cheesy, tomatoey aroma. With a grin, I told Ken how much I had enjoyed Melo's company.

"We're forming a strong friendship." I kicked off my rubber rain shoes. "I'm promising to pray for healing." I wanted him to be impressed that

I had followed the general precepts of youth ministry. Ken was quiet. I cleared my throat. His silence told me I was not in his favor.

"The last time I prayed with her, I asked God to let me take on her spiritual pain as we did with folks in Pierre." I felt justified doing this ministry work, especially when it was based on his youth ministry model. I hoped he'd be impressed.

"She's got problems, you know, Mary Beth. You'd better watch it." He didn't look at me. He just began eating and wiped his thick blond mustache with a cloth napkin.

He wanted me to meet her, but now I had to be careful. "What do you mean? She is young and innocent and needs a lot of guidance. She talks about you and how what you say in class makes sense." I hung my green raincoat on a hook, hoping my compliment would lift his spirits. Maybe she'd told him about being molested and now he had a problem with her, I thought. "What's going on, Ken?"

He just kept eating. I called the kids to come to dinner, and I shut down. If I couldn't please him, then I just gave up. I was walking on eggshells just like I had while growing up.

After dinner, Chris asked for a candy bar.

Ken yelled at him. "What? We don't eat candy for dessert!" Then he gently lifted Chris onto his lap and whispered, "How about some of Mommy's yummy Boston cream pie that she made last night? It's my favorite." He stood and tucked his button-down shirt into his trousers. "I'll get you some, Chubbs"—his loving nickname for Chris. Ken's trim torso had never changed over the years.

"Melo gives us candy"—Chris's eyes raised to his dad—"sometimes."

Ken stomped out of the kitchen, scowling under his heavy mustache.

I had jumped in headfirst, hoping for God's protection and blessing with my attraction to her. I thought if I kept telling myself it was a case of God's love shining over us, our relationship would be holy. I did not realize then that I was searching deep down in my heart for a strong female to honor me, or maybe for any adult to honor me.

Melo and I prayed together at the beginning and the end of our session. After months of weekly meetings, we got to know each other. Then we went deeper, and our connection grew tight. I was caring and protective, and she was strong and needed "taming" like the fox in *The Little Prince*. This was how the youth ministry ran back in Pierre. An adult befriended some-one and slowly made a trusting, lasting friendship. But I could not stop my thoughts from going elsewhere. Like how her muscular legs looked in those shorts she liked to wear after lacrosse practice.

Chapter 5

Melo and I met in my living room while Paul napped; she curled up in my flowered chair and reminisced about how her family had forgotten her tenth birthday. Her loose-fitting jeans had holes everywhere, like they had been washed many times. The downy-white threads feathered out from the frayed openings.

My birthday was never forgotten, but I often felt invisible because of the arguing in my childhood home. Growing up in the fifties and sixties throttled me. Mom had told me men were better than women in every profession.

"What about cooking?" I asked at age twelve.

"Men are better. The most famous are the French chefs."

Nuns served the priests. Women could not be a part of Mass. There were no altar girls. Men dominated every profession. The Equal Rights Amendment didn't pass. The Moral Majority claimed that if it passed, men and women would have to use the same bathroom. My friend Leanne was devastated that women still didn't have equal rights. From movies, I gathered that women were meant to adore men and worship their knowledge and influence. My goal was to find a man who could be, and do, marvelous things for me.

Melo told me about a sexual relationship she'd had with her roommate and how this made her feel troubled in her Christianity. My only knowledge of gay people was from Anita Bryant; I knew gay people could not adopt. Ken's doctor friend, Larry, said that a gay person could get cured of their sexual orientation if they chose to be cured.

Is Melo gay? Should I try to cure her? I knew that no matter what she said or did, I would remain faithful to her as a mentor, and thus rationalized that I would still be her friend. One of my many Ken-appointed Christian counselors was from Colorado. Dr. Larry and Ken had sent me there for a week two years prior. I checked in by phone with that same Colorado counselor. She said to hold onto the friendship and not to abandon Melo. It was almost a godsend that my friendship with Melo was blessed by a Ken-approved, Ken-appointed counselor, so I tried to relax. But I felt guilty because I had not told my counselor how intense my feelings were for Melo. I was certain God would show me what to say.

I heard a noise at the back door. "Who's that?"

Melo's eyes darted to the doorway.

I turned around in my chair. It was Ken. His blue eyes examined the room.

"Don't you have a class starting right now?" I pointed to my watch.

"I forgot something." He vanished up the stairs. In a minute, he appeared back down and slammed the screen door. "I won't be back until dinner."

I was on edge for the rest of the visit. Ken had always monitored my relationships with others—male and female.

I remembered the time he'd come home from a five-day trip and noticed the contraceptive foam was in a different spot. He dug around in the top drawer of our bedroom chest of drawers. "Why is the foam over here instead of over there?" he'd said, pointing to both sides of the deep drawer.

I had just looked at him with my brow furrowed.

"Did you have sex with that neighbor down the street?" he'd accused me.

I blew out a big exhale. I raised my voice, stood, and said, "Because when I put clean laundry in the drawer, I shove it to the other side! Get a grip, Ken!" With that, I had stormed out of the bedroom.

Melo was unaware of my agitation at Ken's unexpected appearance. I did not say a word.

As the weeks went on, so did our deep intimacy. I experienced a physical pull to Melo. Our kinetic relationship expanded, especially with our letters about how God would protect us in our love for each other because the Bible said we were to love God first and love others as we love ourselves. Three times a week when we jogged with others, I gave her a prayer note.

Dear Melo,

I love our time together. Our relationship is healing and soothing to me. I look forward to seeing you each time. You have
given me so much; you give light to my dark mornings. Your
energy is a magnet for me.

Love in Jesus,

Mary Beth

Each morning, I found myself glancing up from my antique desk in
front of the window, often during my Bible-reading time, to see when she
would come out of the woods next door to our house.

Ken read his Bible in his upstairs office while the kids were still asleep.
I admired how much he read and what he read. He was an avid reader of
spiritual books and conservative magazines.

The morning was my time to exercise since I was home all day with
Paul. I hurried to greet the smell of sovereignty Melo brought. I wished
I could be as free as she was. My year in Paris was the only time I was
queen for a day, every day. I'd felt free in Paris. No rules, no parents, and
no Catholic church. I could go anywhere on the metro for twenty cents. No
one gave me permission to do, say, or be. Everything took my breath away,
just like Melo. In her world, she reigned. When she smiled at me, her neck
turned red. She said it was because she was full of emotion. With her, I felt
accepted and important.

Eleven years previous, within the first year of my marriage, I had found
out Ken loved another woman. I had no self-care tools. He gave me no
information on what went on between him and his secretary. I went into
a depression. It was a wounding event. At only twenty-two years of age,
newly married, I believed I shared my marriage with another woman. I lost
my admiration for him. That entire year, I cried, smoked cigarettes, and
agonized alone about how unimportant I felt. I thought that if people felt
sorry for me, things would change. It goes with the Catholic long-suffering

soul. "Oh, poor Mary Beth, she had an ogre on her tail. What a saint!" As a victim, I thought I got sympathy and could blame others for my problems. I soon learned that blaming is a codependent behavior. I played the victim throughout the marriage, and what a miserable way it was to be.

Melo was positive. She laughed and joked and was serious. Breaking rules, she looked at me like I was her end-all. When I looked at her, I saw who I wanted to be. All my life, I looked for people I wanted to emulate, people I could mirror: my best friends, Ken, people who lived in colonial homes, and then Melo.

"Come in a sec," I said to her.

We hugged for an extra-long time so I could get the outdoor whiff of morning dew on her clothing and skin. She smelled like fresh sheets on the line.

She handed me a note of her latest, deepest prayer feelings. Even her handwriting gave me a flutter. Her letters had a passion and a declaration of love for me and for God. Besides praying in person when we got together, we also wrote out the prayers we said in our heads. I stuck the note in my purse on the counter to read later.

She had just gotten herself an eighties perm. "Yeah, now I look like Richard Simmons!" she said with a laugh. She did not seem to care outwardly about hairstyles. I liked that about her. The tight curls lifted her forehead and barely covered her ears.

She watched as I sat down to tie my sneakers on the basket-weave-tiled floor. She looked at me like I was the most important person in the world.

"I have a rock in my sneaker," she said.

"Here, let me look at your foot." She sat on the bench lengthwise, and I rubbed her foot. I knew then that I had crossed a line, but I hid under the blanket of Christian friendship. It wasn't the touch that crossed the line; it was my deep emotions for her. "Does that tickle?"

She let out a long breath, her neck flushed. "No, it feels good."

Chapter 6

It had been a week since I saw Melo. Today was mentor day. It was a beautiful, mild March morning. In Pierre, we usually still had piles of snow and snowstorms at this time of year.

Upstairs, I could hear Ken's muffled voice murmuring, but I could not decipher who he was talking to. I'd later learn he was talking to Dr. Larry, his Christian mentor, fundraiser, and friend in Pierre who had become associated with Ken and his youth ministry. After hanging up, he bounded down the stairs from his office, leaned close to me, and in a deep voice said, "Today, you will *not* contact Melo," his minty mouthwash breath in my face.

I released my arm from his clasp. "But I have already made bird-watching plans with her and another student." I was intentionally trying to do things with her that included others. As an expert at pleasing others, I knew deep down his opinion of Melo was going south. I stepped away from him and put the raspberry-jelly toast on Gabrielle's plate.

"Cancel it!" His voice rose in anger.

Gabrielle flinched. Paul bellowed in the highchair, holding his "mahgee," a tattered blue-and-white remnant of his baby blanket, close to his face. I picked him up and held him close to me. "Come here, sweetheart." I put his cheek to mine and sang a French song that always made him smile. "*Un éléphant, qui se promenait, tout doucement, dans la forêt . . .*" I rocked him. I had no appetite. Ken's stare pierced me. I put Paul back in the highchair.

"Give me back my car!" Chris pointed to the tiny red sports car Gabrielle was holding.

"I'm just looking at it, stupid!" She threw it at him.

Gabrielle's heart-shaped face scrutinized us. I silently marched into the living room, took a deep breath in with six counts, then exhaled, returned, and finished feeding Chris and Paul.

Before leaving, Ken gently approached Gabrielle and said, "Mommy and I are working on some hard stuff. Everything will be all right, sweetheart." She leaned into his chest while he kissed the top of her head.

I worried about the damage we were inflicting on our children. I remembered how I felt when my parents would fight in front of me. Ken and I had been yelling at each other for the whole eleven years of our life together, even before we were married.

He went back to his classes. I started making scrambled eggs for Paul after the older two went upstairs to play. I knew what I was doing with Melo. I desperately wanted her in my life, and I wanted the marriage too. The butter melted in the fry pan on the stove. I whipped two eggs and water with a fork. But I was not willing to admit that the love I felt for Melo had grown to such intensity. I shook out parmesan cheese from a green container onto the eggs and poured it all into the buttery pan. I was lying to myself.

After I finished the dishes and canceled a sitter, Melo showed up in front of the house in her brown Toyota to go bird-watching. I walked to her car and leaned into the window. She looked up at me and winked. "Hey!"

"Hi, Melo—I guess I'm not going. Ken's forbidding me."

"Forbidding?! What is this, the Dark Ages?" she snapped.

I teared up and poured out what I had been withholding from her since we met.

"Ken is . . . he's angry all the time lately."

"About what?" She gripped the steering wheel and shifted in her seat.

"He thinks we're . . . doing something bad. He doesn't like us hanging out together."

Melo's lips curled inward. "I feel betrayed by him, Mary Beth. He promised that he would be there for me forever. I don't understand. He called me a healer." She put her hand over her face, got out of the car, and wiped her tears.

Chris ran out to look in her pockets for candy. She smiled at him, put her hand on his head, turned, and left in her car.

I desperately wanted the company of Melo and another student; I had never been bird-watching. I don't know if Ken checked up on me or if he just knew I would obey his orders, but we never talked about what I did or did not do that day.

Chapter 7

"Why are you talking to everyone on campus about Melo and me?"

"I want to save our marriage, Mary Beth. It's my duty as a Christian husband." He sat on the edge of our king-sized bed and put his hands on his bowed head.

"I am here, and Ken, I have no plans of going anywhere else." I straightened the blue-paisley Priscilla curtains and dumped a basket of laundry on the bed.

"I received a phone call from the English professor's wife. She wanted to have coffee together and talk to me about how she deals with her boundaries with students." I paused. He didn't look at me. "Did you set that up?" I picked up and folded the embroidered dish towel. It said *Tuesday* and depicted a woman ironing.

"Mary Beth, look, you are jeopardizing our marriage with this student. I'm only trying—"

"*You* are jeopardizing our marriage, Ken. Melo told me that in class you brought up the evils of homosexuality and warned your students about friendships that are unhealthy. This is getting way out of hand!" I threw the towel back to the pile of clothes on the bed. "Don't you *dare* go around this campus talking about me and Melo!"

"I do what I have to do," he said dismissively as he walked into his office.

I tiptoed past Paul's room, stuck my head into his office, and muted my voice through my teeth. "The theology professor told me that you are talking to the vice president of the college about us."

I slammed his door. I did not see a way out. My nightmares were always of being cornered. In the nightmares, I was in a deep hole and a gorilla at the top prevented my leaving. Ken knew how much I cared about what other people thought of me. I made decisions based on how I'd look in other people's eyes. All I knew was that I wanted her in my life no matter what.

I kept denying what Ken saw in my face, my actions, and my heart. He could recognize my behaviors because he'd loved his secretary during the first year of our marriage.

I broke a cardinal rule, only married for three months and home alone in Pierre with no job. Our basement apartment had two bedrooms. One was Ken's office. I went to his desk, opened the drawer carefully, and pulled out his private journal. The cucumber smell of the thick white pages offered a precious quality to the notebook. The unlined page revealed the sexy curves of Ken's handwriting; the cursive that wrote love notes in books he gave me. Looking for love words about me, I skimmed the last few pages. My eyes abruptly locked onto the words, *"I love two women. How can I work through this, Lord?"*

I confronted him. He denied any wrongdoing.

That first year, my thoughts had spiraled around Ken loving two women. I began smoking; even Ken smoked. I became so miserable that year, I felt I had nothing to live for. But after he had that affair, or "loved two women," as he called it, he'd been jealous, probably afraid I would do what he did. In Pierre, he accused me of having sex with the neighbor man I had befriended and forbade me to have a female friend whose spirituality was too universal for him.

That same year, Dr. Larry talked to me alone and saw how distraught I was. He and Ken decided together that our marriage wouldn't make it unless his secretary, Pauline, was removed like a pawn. Ken never told me, and I didn't ask what exactly he and Pauline did when they were alone. I just sat with it while feeling the pain of sharing my husband, the man I idealized, with another woman. He even gathered a meeting of leaders, committee folks, and staff to tell them he had gone too far with his secretary, so she was sent to the Minneapolis ministry. I remember sitting in the background, unable to give input, wondering how my husband was explaining to his staff what he had done. He certainly hadn't explained anything to me.

Ken and Dr. Larry had decided I was the problem. They put me on antidepressants, and Pauline, his secretary, was sent to live in Minneapolis. Pauline was innocent, tender, and very easily manipulated. She was like me. She worked for him. She was one of his leaders and did whatever he asked. What a power rush that must have been for him, for all men at that time, to have sweet young things at their disposal. He never once told me what happened between them nor where she was sent in Minneapolis. I wondered if they talked on the phone when Ken needed to contact his boss who lived in Minneapolis. *Did he have contact with her when he went for regional meetings there?*

The only thing he would admit was that it was an affair of the heart. Years later, my sister Lucy told me Pauline had confessed to her that the relationship had been physical. I didn't want to believe that. I couldn't. How could I stay married if he'd been unfaithful?

I felt desperate then, constantly wondering if he and Pauline were together at his office. I imagined them talking and embracing late into the evening. Something had broken inside me when I discovered his affair. My mind flashed back to times during that year, 1972, before I read his journal, when he and Pauline were holding hands and crying face to face at a conference in Colorado. On the ride back, they were in an argumentative silence. They were fighting like spouses, so I offered her the front seat. I did not battle him like he was doing to me because I trusted him. My style was to withdraw and descend into depression. I blocked that memory and took one forward step at a time as a wife and mother. I had no plan B.

Heat flushed through my body remembering the pain.

The "one-way gate" for me was Ken's love for another woman. It had changed everything. I had stuffed away the pain of his affair, thinking her being gone would heal me. But I didn't realize until years later that his affair had changed my love for him and that he couldn't come back into my heart. The gate had closed.

When the kids were little in Pierre, I tried to make a home. I cooked French foods, had babies, and sewed costumes for them for Halloween. My children kept me busy, and being the supportive minister's wife was a full-time job. I led Bible studies, did some public speaking to Christian organizations, and led women's groups.

It was exciting having my own dance business in our newly purchased second Pierre home.

"This family room is perfect for a dance studio, Mary Beth!" Ken suggested as we walked through a split-level home that was for sale in Pierre. "Look, and the students could access the studio through the garage service door!"

Looking around the house, I started to imagine my office next to the laundry room and the huge bathroom for the students to change.

"I like it, Ken!" I agreed. "These windows are perfect. I can put a barre right here under it." My hand gestured under the window.

"And then you won't have to go to the 'Y' to teach."

Ken and I embraced. He wanted me to be successful. "Thank you, Ken, I love this idea. And I love it when you give me all your attention." I put my arms around his neck and kissed him. "Let's buy it!"

I walked into the bathroom. "What do you think? Could we put shelves in here?" I pointed to the bare wall.

He put his hand on his cleft chin. "Yes, I can make simple cubby-hole shelves, like this." He made a square with his finger on the wall. "And hooks for their coats underneath."

Five years into our marriage, we bought our second house and made the level eight steps down from the living room into a dance studio with a piano, mirrors, and barres. I hung my Degas poster of dancers tying their toe shoes. Ken took black-and-white student-dancer photos and developed them for hanging. The studio made me happy. My business grew to a hundred students a week. The joy of creating each class lasted for six years, until we decided to move to Rhode Island.

Two-year-old Chris in his diapers and red leotards, and five-year-old Gabrielle in a swirly skirt, danced to Vivaldi in the studio before bedtime, while Ken sat on the carpeted steps and watched us.

"I have two invisible ladybugs, and we're going to give them each a fun ride in the palms of our hands." I tenderly gave an invisible ladybug to each student. They carefully carried a cupped hand to the center of the studio. Then I put a Tchaikovsky record on the turntable, and we danced, giving the imaginary ladybugs the rides of their lives.

That's how I used to dance in my dreams as a little girl. I fantasized about myself on a stage or in a musical as I kicked my skirts and twirled across the floor. My arms tried to swoop up every bit of space around me. It felt like sliding through butter. I was the star dancer, and my imaginary viewers wanted to see my every move under the spotlight.

The pre-ballet classes enjoyed props, invisible and otherwise, to engage their imaginations. My philosophy was that if a child was comfortable in her body and how she moved, then she developed the self-confidence to be a leader. I easily found success teaching pre-ballet and ballet. I took older students to ballet performances in Minneapolis. Ken made sure I put any extra money I earned in a savings account for the kids. He kept the passbook and control of the money. I was able to squeeze out shoes for the kids, a subscription to *Dance Magazine*, and dancewear for me.

I believe I grew out of love, or out of admiration, with him. No longer did my heart skip a beat at his deep voice or his long, blond sideburns. My gaze no longer lingered on his hairy forearms and wide hands. I no longer waited for his wisdom on what a Bible verse meant. He was no longer my rock star.

My love for Melo smothered any logic I had, or any sympathy I felt for Ken. His actions disgusted me. He was no longer attractive to me. His face was always angry, his fingers constantly pointing.

The college, the Christians, and my dream home became a fence that locked me in.

I had hoped to raise my children and spend a long life in my cedar-sided colonial. And with a teaching job, I would be the professor's wife who had a career. This home symbolized permanency. I felt my home would protect me and take care of me. It was a sign of wealth and stature, which I thought was attached only to Ken.

I went back to my mantra. I was an expert at mantras. One was "divorce is not an option." Another was "I am only loving Melo with Christian love." I didn't realize then that both mantras were inaccurate.

I knew I had secret inappropriate thoughts. But no one knew about them. If I did not talk about them, I thought I could make them go away. Gossip spread throughout the campus. People in the town were choosing sides.

Chapter 8

Ken made plans to send me away for spiritual counseling at a monastery in New Hampshire. Sister Margaret, our mentor, referred us to the monastery. I trusted her opinion. She told me before I left that I would like Brother Gerald. She assured me that the protocol at the monastery when meeting with someone was to not hear any opinions from the spouse beforehand. Ken had been sneaky about this in the past, so I was still a bit leery that he would interfere with my time at the monastery, making me the problem. But I was optimistic that this Brother Gerald would work some miracle in our marriage.

Through the past eleven years, whenever Ken and I had marriage difficulties, he and Dr. Larry would send me away, as though I were the problem. After Ken's affair with Pauline, antidepressants sounded good to me. Ken and Dr. Larry also introduced me to biofeedback, which helped me with anxiety and taught me to calm my breathing.

The youth ministry was interdenominational. As the official youth leader in Pierre, Ken and Dr. Larry were like the heads of the "church." They did not adhere to any specific denomination. My mindset was to do as they suggested because they were men and leaders, and I thought they knew more than me and had better connections with the right people. They were like the "elders." I admired Dr. Larry as a medical doctor and a man of wisdom. After I went to Colorado and Minneapolis to see Christian therapists, my unhappiness didn't change. The next solution they tried was to send me away for a long weekend in New Hampshire.

A haven retreat in a monastery sounded like an oasis. I looked forward to getting away from Ken and the screaming. We traveled as a family up north and arrived at a quaint castle-like compound surrounded by red spruces and white birch trees. The spring air smelled fresh.

I exited the van, stretching.

"Mommy is going to stay here and pray during the long weekend, kids." I heard Ken's singsong voice from inside the camper van.

He sounded so relieved, and that surprised me. It was a respite for him too, from the arguing. So far, the kids just accepted whatever he said. They did look to me for cues, but I did not voice my opinions because I didn't want them to feel conflicted. I leaned in the window and smiled at the three of them.

"It'll just be for a few days. Gabrielle, can you help your daddy?"

Her dark bangs clumped on her forehead, and she seemed smaller than usual, sitting on the camper bench seat, but she nodded back. Chris had fallen asleep next to her. I tucked my hair behind my ears and bent to kiss them. "I love you guys."

"But who will sleep with me till I fall asleep?" Paul whined.

"I will, Paul." Ken sent a smile to our youngest. "Daddy wants a turn to put you to bed."

"Can I sit in front, Daddy, for the ride home?" Chris asked, suddenly awake.

"No!" Gabrielle complained. "I'm the oldest."

Ken handed me my suitcase and hugged me. "Enjoy the quiet–wish I were joining you." He nodded in the direction of the kids.

I waved until they disappeared down the hill in the green VW, then picked up my suitcase and headed toward the castle.

After a tour of the dining room and sitting area, I was shown my tiny room with soaring ceilings. Every room had a fireplace. It was chilly, and I could smell the burnt ash from a recent fire. People were pleasant, smiling as we passed, and I could already feel the tension in my body loosening.

Brother Gerald met me in his narrow office. It had twelve-foot ceilings and one small window. He was a thin man with short blond hair combed forward. He didn't wear "monk robes," but instead leaned back in his chair in a long-sleeve flannel shirt and jeans.

After we shared stories about our common friend, Sister Margaret, he smiled at me and leaned forward.

"Tell me about your childhood."

Studying the bare yellow plaster walls with exposed white patches where the plaster had peeled, I wondered where to begin. What should I reveal to this man who I did not know? I trusted Sister Margaret's advice and the belief in sharing with clergy, a practice I had grown up with. Talking about your most intimate details, your sins, and your successes with a man of the cloth was a way to peace of mind and heart. So, I began with Dad's drinking and Mom's anger, the two rhythms of my growing-up years that made our whole family walk on eggshells.

He listened and nodded occasionally, keeping his eyes on me. He did not flinch at my descriptions. The more I talked, the more I felt visible; it was so different from my dad, who did not make eye contact, and my mom, whose critical looks bore into me. This guy, I was sure, would give me some answers on how to proceed. I heard no footsteps or sounds. The hushed monastery surroundings felt like a womb.

"Sounds like it was hard being the oldest in your angry family, Mary Beth. And in high school?" He lit a patchouli candle. "How did you manage?"

"I was depressed, I think. I had pimples and hid them under greasy bangs. All I wanted was to be a cheerleader, so people would notice me." My finger twirled a strand of hair. "I wanted to be loved. I let one boy make out with me and touch me from the waist up while we dated. I made out with many other boys."

He asked questions about my parents' involvement in the John Birch Society, an anti-communist organization with conspiracy theories. I told him how I tried to please everyone, even the priests and nuns at my Catholic high school, and especially my parents. I thought that happiness for people around me was easy as long as I pleased them, which meant I could never say what I was thinking, because if I said the wrong thing, I thought everything would topple down. I treaded guardedly.

The sunlight from the high window came down in an oblique line to the crucifix hanging on the wall. Brother Gerald shifted in his chair, lighting another cigarette.

"A pretty conservative background, Mary Beth. Right?"

"One of those priests that came to the John Birch meetings chose the Catholic women's college that I attended."

His eyes widened. "You didn't choose your college?"

"I didn't. I obeyed. I was afraid to give my opinion of Middlebury, Vermont, or Grand Rapids, Michigan, for the French programs. Deep down, I couldn't express my wants and desires. What I wished for most was for others to love me. Therefore, as you can see, I tried to please whoever was in charge." I stared down at my empty hands. "That priest also told me not to be on the homecoming court, but it was up to me to decide. So, I dropped out." I bit the skin on my finger. "My first year in college, I gained weight and stayed at the library on Fridays studying late. I was lonely and shy."

"That's understandable, even normal, I think."

"I wanted out. Out of my family, out of that college, out of the rules that governed my life. During the summer, I sat in the Pierre Library and researched colleges that had a junior year abroad for the same price. So, I found a college program abroad that was comparable in price and traveled to live in Paris for a full year."

He looked impressed. "Did your parents go along with it?"

"My mom objected, but I pushed hard like I never had before."

"Did you find freedom in Paris?"

"That year in Paris was life-changing for me."

He smiled at that, as if it were a joke, then looked at his watch. "Let's talk more after lunch."

I was exhausted and welcomed the break. I ate a white-fish lunch alone and thought about what I had told him. It was nice having his undivided attention. I sat in my room with my notebook in hand and wrote a prayer for my retreat time and my life: *Dear Jesus, Make the screaming go away in my marriage. Let me find a way to enjoy my beautiful home and children. Protect them from the yelling. Thank you for Brother Gerald and his acceptance of me and my past.*

We continued our conversation after lunch.

"Tell me about Paris, *s'il te plaît.*" He grinned. "I know some French."

I was more relaxed with him than I had been that morning. I pulled a cardigan over my shoulders and curled my feet under my legs. "First of all, I accepted Jesus into my life back with Ken in Pierre. Then, in France, I wrote out my prayers every day on bits of paper in tiny penmanship. I woke up every day excited to explore a new part of Paris with my city map and student Métro pass. It was my big escape from being told what to do. I took risks."

He smiled.

"I traveled by train and by plane, and hitchhiked to neighboring countries. Paris was a life raft. I existed unmanaged by authority figures. I soaked in my surroundings and submerged myself into another culture and language. The Pierre culture of possessing and repressing wasn't valid in my life then. Immersion in another culture and language reprogrammed me. But a year wasn't enough. I only tasted freedom. I remember saying to myself that if I died tomorrow, I felt that I would have lived my life to the fullest. I had the autonomy to do what I wanted and to be who I was meant to be without restraint.

"I danced at the *Schola Cantorum de Paris*. My eyes opened to the world, to my first sexual experience, to politics, to class systems. It was quite different than Pierre and Winona, where my college was. I fell in love." I did not tell Gerald that unprotected sex produced a miscarriage while still in Europe. Unfortunately, I had not tried even a sip of French wine.

He nodded and rested back in his chair with his hand under his chin.

"When I came home from my year in Paris, Ken reappeared in my life and snatched me up! He sent me some spiritual books while I was in France, but I didn't get them."

"Did you feel attracted to him?" He flicked cigarette ash into the cutglass ashtray on his desk. I was amazed he was still attentive, listening so carefully.

"I did. He was the one who introduced me to a deeper spiritual life. Plus, when he kissed me, I could think of no one else. He was the answer to everything in my life. His penetrating eyes drew me in to want to know everything about how he thought and what he read. For me, he was unusual in that he introduced a whole new ethos of seeing the world. His ideas floored me. I felt safe around him. My attraction to him was about more than looks. I couldn't get enough of him, his heart and mind. I might have put Ken on the same level as God. After I caught my breath, I went back to Winona for my senior year in college. Ken lived in Pierre." I did not know if Gerald would understand the born-again Christian stuff, but he did not flinch.

We talked a little more and quit for the day. By evening, I felt a bit lighter inside. The castle was bereft of other humans, as if it were inhabited by just me and this priest. I explored the rooms next to mine and found the kitchen. I went to the refrigerator as instructed to find my dinner. The room was a long, wide rectangle. A worn wooden table the size of two outdoor tables filled the center of the kitchen. The shelved walls held assorted sizes of crocks and jars. I sat in silence, chewing slowly as I ate a roast beef sandwich.

On the second day, we met again and Brother Gerald started with my marriage. I began to tell him what was going on with me and Ken. I told him about my ballet studio, how it gave me my power, how Ken encouraged me, and how it began to blossom.

"I felt invisible many times during our married life," I said. "But this gave me a sense of self, and I began making money from teaching dance. That was six years into our marriage, only six years ago. Ken kept a tight rein on my income. He made sure I put most of it into savings and then he kept control of the passbook accounts."

Brother Gerald waited while I sat for a moment, biting my lip, wondering how to continue. His silence was encouraging, so I pushed on. I disclosed Ken's affair with Pauline and the first physical fight, witnessed by Gabrielle.

Brother Gerald handed me a tissue box, and I blew my nose. "Did you ever feel like leaving?"

"Yes. After that horrible fight in front of Gabrielle, I took some change and went to a motel a mile away. I asked the clerk if I could stay overnight for seven dollars. I also asked if I could hide my car in the back."

Gerald leaned forward.

"Then, Ken forbade me to study Koine Greek with a friend in Pierre because her theology was too universal. He has controlled me and who I spend time with for most of our marriage. Now, here we are in Rhode Island, and he wants my friendship with Melo, a student of his, to cease," I said, raising my voice.

He nodded once. "This is hard stuff. I must pray about it. Let's stop for now."

I was exhausted and agreed. My big secret was out—I had talked about Melo. "I'm thinking of inviting Melo to visit tomorrow. Is that OK?"

He gave a long look, then nodded. I guess that he wanted me to make the decision instead of getting permission. There was going to be an anniversary celebration the next evening, so there would be many people in the monastery.

Later that evening, I went to the monastery office and called Melo collect to invite her to visit. It was bliss just to hear her voice. But she sounded doubtful.

"But what about Ken? He's already called several times to make sure I'm still here working at the switchboard."

I could not believe it. He was tracking her, just as he stalked me. I tried to keep the anger out of my voice. "Just come for a quick visit," I told her. "And you can be back before your next shift."

Chapter 9

On the third day, I told Brother Gerald that Melo was coming. He did not condone nor condemn.

She made the two-hour drive in her faded brown Toyota Camry. I was thrilled to be around her without restraints and accusations. After my last session with Brother Gerald, I waited in the dim hearth room and then stood at the door. Dusk was approaching as I bit the skin around my nails. When I stepped outside, I buttoned my white cardigan. The lights of her car turned off; my pulse quickened. We reached for each other, laughing. Squeezing her and pressing her cheek next to mine, I inhaled her aroma of white pine. Melo was smiling. I breathed quietly into her ear.

"Je t'aime, ma petite poulette."

She did not know what I said but had a big enduring smile. It was mind-boggling to have her all to myself for a few hours. We went to my simple room, sat on the single bed, and leaned back against the wall.

"My heart feels full," I said.

"I'm just happy to be here with you, Mary Beth." She inhaled.

I was not used to being around her without looking over my shoulder, and I wanted to cherish this moment.

I told her about my conversations with Brother Gerald. I specifically told her about Ken throwing pottery at me in front of Gabrielle.

"He didn't like that I was learning Greek to analyze the translations of certain words in the New Testament, so he lunged toward me."

"What! Oh, Mare."

"It was that I challenged him. I cringed at the end of the slate counter next to the plastic mat under Chris's highchair where bits of oatmeal and yogurt collected. Ken reached to the corner of the countertop where I had my favorite pieces of Deneen pottery nestled one inside the other. That pottery was a treasured gift from Dad. One by one, Ken threw the pieces at me, wild eyed and yelling."

Melo shook her head with a frown.

"Crouching, I felt my heart pound. He charged to where I squatted. He glowered at me. I clutched the countertop that I had happily picked out at the store a year earlier.

"I was miserable about the matching pieces of blue and white that were scattered on the counter and floor. I turned to my four-year-old daughter, who stood in the doorway. Her feet were turned out, and her soft pigtails looked like little shells bouncing lopsided above her ears. Her facial expression brought me to a complete stop. She started crying and yelled at us to stop fighting. I tried to veil the fact that Gabrielle had seen her dad throw pottery bowls at me. I gathered her in my arms and put her head on my shoulders to hide her eyes from the painful mess and the uncertainty on my face." I wiped my eyes.

Melo's face was somber. "That makes me mad. She was too little to see that kind of violence." She leaned forward with her elbows on her knees. "And what about you? That must have been traumatic."

"I went numb, Melo. I didn't know what to do. I just kept hoping and praying that things would get better. But I felt powerless then."

Melo looked at me intently. "Mare? I'm sorry that happened to you." She continued to look pensive.

"I feel more powerful when I'm with you."

There was a twentieth-anniversary celebration for one of the monks that night in the monastery. We each were presented with a glass of champagne and invited to go through a buffet. Melo loved being with me in the monastery even though she didn't know anyone there. We laughed and talked and held each other tenderly on the bed for hours into the night. Thoughts of touching her kept running through my mind. I was conflicted. I wanted her close, her body, her breath, her touch. My mind blocked out anything else. Then I finally asked.

"Will you do something for me?"

"OK."

"Will you kiss me fifteen times?" She kissed my face and arms many times, then sat up.

"Would you do something for me?" she asked me. I nodded.

"Let me do it again."

Before her mouth touched my skin, I reached for her face and looked into her eyes. "Would you kiss me everywhere? Except, you know, not there." My silky pink nightgown clung to me as she lay on top of me. She kissed my face. She slowly and carefully kissed my eyes and cheeks, my nose, eyebrows, and my chin. I knew I was adored. I pulled her up to face me. My arms were around her, and we fell asleep for a few minutes. When I awoke, I wondered what I was doing. I slept on the small bed, and she slept on the floor for the rest of the night, which appeased me somewhat. In the morning, we had to hurry to get her back to the switchboard job before my husband would notice her absence.

We went to separate stalls to take showers. "Do you have any soap?" I asked. My desire to see her naked mounted; I went into her stall for soap and touched her breast in the shower. She smiled at me and shyly looked down. We said nothing, finished our showers, and dried off for the day. I had crossed a line, but I still tried to justify it as normal behavior. I know now that my behavior was inappropriate and hurtful to Ken. But I reined in my denial. It was something I was good at. As a child, I had pretended along with my family that we were an upstanding family in Pierre. In my marriage, I lived the same pretense to feel safe.

After leaving later that morning, Melo got lost and called me from a phone booth, crying because she would not make it in time to go back to work. She asked me what to do. My strength moved in where Melo's dropped. I told her to call in sick and come back to the monastery. We regrouped and got her directions straight.

Her hope was intoxicating. I tried to believe the things she said and push my own doubts away; I was optimistic when I listened to her words. Her positivity let me breathe fully instead of holding my breath and clenching my jaw. But I knew she was repeating encouraging words to make even herself feel better.

"I am so happy to be here with you at this moment. I'm not going to let anything ruin this time." We had exchanged many kisses and held each other for hours the night before. My deep fears were rising. I didn't know how I going to keep the lid on this boiling pot.

Chapter 10

After the car ride back from New Hampshire, wherein Ken had been unusually quiet, I tended to the kids and Ken escaped to his office. I could hear him upstairs on the phone constantly. Other than sniping at each other about trivial things, we ignored each other with the silent treatment. We exchanged no talk of feelings. We didn't even argue. And he did not question me about Melo's absence at the switchboard. He only asked a few surface questions about the retreat. I guessed that he suspected Melo had come and he was calculating a strategic time to confront me. For the time being, I was relieved.

When I wrote at my desk the next morning, I took my journal off the bookcase next to my desk to write down my prayers for the day. I did not write of my sexual feelings for Melo in my prayer journal; I still had not admitted those feelings to myself. I could openly pray for her and not hide that.

Today I am thankful for this beautiful planet, for my family, for Melo. Help me to listen to what you, Jesus, are saying to me in this dilemma I face. Let Ken understand my heart and open his. Protect the kids. Give me wisdom in my choices for today.

The morning sun peeked onto my desk, making pink and blue hues through the hanging stained glass. Ken came downstairs from his office, interrupting his Bible study time, holding an empty cup of tea. I could smell the Constant Comment tea bag that was wrapped around his spoon. He stood silently in his moccasins and blue morning jacket, looking over my shoulder at what I was writing.

"What are you doing, Ken?" I said as I lifted my journal to my chest.

"I have every right to know what my wife is writing about." At the sound of his low, gravelly voice and the presence of his index finger too close to my face, I recoiled and set the journal down. The morning joy I used to see in his face was gone. His forehead was bunched in ripples.

"Are you kidding?" My hands jerked in the air.

I stormed from the glass-topped desk with my journal and went to the backyard to have a cigarette. I was smoking more often. Sitting on the picnic table with my feet on the bench, elbows perched on my knees, I did not care what Christian rule I broke by smoking. Catholics smoked, but not the born-again Christian Moral Majority. I felt guilty about lying with Melo in my nightgown up at the monastery, not to mention taking in all her kisses. But I told myself they were not sexual because we had refrained from kissing on the lips. I justified touching her breast as being curious. This was my first experience with loving a woman. I was not sure of the boundaries—at least, I did not admit to myself where those boundaries were. And I used that ambiguity to my advantage. Men see each other naked all the time in showers. After crushing the cigarette, I flicked it and jumped off the picnic table. I went back inside.

"I need alone time. I'm going to sit on Narragansett Beach by myself and pray, meditate, and write," I announced boldly. I gathered my journal, my pillows, and the orange-and-yellow afghan my sister had crocheted.

I got no argument from Ken.

I loved that beach for many reasons. I even liked its pungent smell of dead shellfish. It was only a five-minute drive by car. The waves left a foot-wide row of small rocks, shells, and limply scattered dark-green seaweed on the sandy shore. Every so often, an invisible ship in the distance sounded its foghorn. It was a wonderful place to be alone. I sprawled out on my stomach, one leg at each corner of my side of the afghan, my pillow and notebook at the other end, as if it were my private space. The beach was serene and quiet, the sun hidden behind the gray sky. The watery swish of the waves and a slight breeze put me to sleep for a while. When I woke, I thought of Melo and wondered what she might be doing at that instant. I wrote a letter to her. I had to be careful not to say too much in case Ken got ahold of it.

Melo, my Melo!

I miss you already. I am alone and thinking about you and our special time. I know God will bless our love and keep it pure and safe. I will love you as long as the yellow star that I told you about is traveling toward the earth. Nothing can separate us.

Mary Beth

I wanted her kisses and love letters. I would be fine with just those two things. In my notebook, I conjured up these rationalizations: women hold hands in many countries. I touched a breast, and breasts are touched inadvertently all the time. Kisses are energy-giving, tender gestures. Europeans give kisses as greetings daily. I avoided genitals and lip or tongue make-out sessions. My love letters were smothered in God's love and approval. All these rationalizations justified my previous actions and thoughts. I lay back again on my pillow and looked up into the sunless sky. I heard a seagull. As I lay still, sandpipers slowly walked stick legged into the water, picking at crustaceans on the shore with their long beaks.

This was the Rhode Island I loved and wanted to wrap myself around. I relished the varied languages I had heard, the Italian influence on food and politics, and the vats of live lobsters. I adored being on the East Coast, which seemed like another country, far different from the Pierre of less than a year ago. In France, I remembered the open markets and fresh fish everywhere. Art was abundant in France. The landscaping, architecture, and food had all been laid out artistically as they were in Rhode Island. On the East Coast, there was so much access to a greater world.

In the beginning, I had worshiped Ken too much and given him too much power. When I met him, he seemed like he could do anything. My world had unlocked with music, the singing at his youth meetings. When he stood next to me singing, I loved hearing his voice unashamedly belt out the words to Dylan or "A Mighty Fortress Is Our God." He impressed me when he played "Imagine" by John Lennon and had his leaders write about their lives. He had opened a deep spiritual life for me. I'd loved him for that. And he was confident in all those areas I wasn't. I had admired him and thought that maybe if he were my husband, I'd have the same confidence. The realization that I could generate my confidence myself was eons from my mind.

We'd started arguing and yelling while we were still engaged. I saw signs of unhappiness from the beginning and ignored them. I was caught in a spiderweb woven by Ken, my rock star. He chose me, not Debra or Jeannie.

I could have canceled the wedding, sent all the bridal shower gifts back, and told the guests it was over. But I would have had to fess up to Mom that not only was she right, but that I didn't know how to manage a canceled wedding. I wanted to be far from Mom's hold and judgment on me. This older man who spoke in tongues and had an out-of-body experience had seemed to have it all together. My ego and the sense of "saving" others had already been wrapped up in a future with Ken.

Geographically, Pierre is in the middle of nowhere. It is isolated, inland, and surrounded by flat plains on all sides for hundreds of miles. Thirty years in that small town suffocated me with small-mindedness and boredom. I always thought I could live more fully in another place. Little did I know then that it wasn't the location, but the man I married and my insecurities that were entrapping me.

While I was sitting there getting ready to close my eyes to pray, I heard voices and a car drive up. The smell of gas overcame my mindfulness.

"Hi, Mommy!" Chris yelled from the car window, the motor still running. The car made tracks on the sand. Chris's straight bangs rolled up in the breeze. I looked past the tall grasses and fence. The sun appeared for a moment, creating stick-like shadows from the vertical board fencing which lined the path to the van.

"Hi, sweetheart." I gave him my warmth, trying to disguise my confusion at hearing his voice. My wide-brimmed hat slightly lifted as I turned to him. "What are you doing here?" I held the brim of my hat. When I saw Ken, my eyes clouded over with disappointment. I looked away to the bay and ignored him.

"We just came to see how you are doing, Mommy!" Chris said with a smile and round eyes. I stood up to face them but stayed on my blanket.

"Well, Chris, I am going to be here a little longer. Is that OK with you, Chris?" He nodded and settled back.

Gabrielle seemed annoyed. "Mom! We came to see what you are doing." Her frowning face retired back into the van.

"Well, Gabrielle, as you can see, I'm just sitting here having some fun by myself." The waves splashed close to me.

I could barely see Paul's eyes peeking over the bottom of the car window.

He started crying. "I want to stay here with Mommy and play in the water!"

Ken consoled him by saying, "No, Paul, Mommy has some things to do without you. She wants to be alone now. Come on kids, let's go!"

Without warning, he drove off with an expressionless face and thin-lipped mouth. Paul cried as they rumbled over the sand onto the asphalt drive. Laying my head down on my blanket, I closed my eyes. My confinement knew no limits and widened now to the sea.

Chapter 11

A few days after my beach day, I stepped soundlessly through the home that I thought would make me happy forever. My fingers ran along the uneven surfaces of the blue-and-white wallpaper in my first formal dining room. I plucked up one of Paul's stray socks under the ladder-back chair and smelled it. A sob coughed from down deep inside while I slid down the wall thinking about the sweet smell of his soft, cushy feet and our story times together. Right in front of me, carrot chunks stuck to the plastic mat under his highchair. The night before, he had sorted them out of the beef stew I made. Our broken marriage was even affecting Paul; I saw him hold his tiny hands over his ears, his generous curls between his fingers while we yelled at each other.

At least Gabrielle had a few serene years before the storm, or did she? She'd seen Ken throwing pottery at me in our Pierre split-level home. She was still taking that new brown pill called Advil for what Ken and his doctor called juvenile rheumatoid arthritis. I was convinced she was manifesting her emotional pain from our battles.

Chris, my middle guy, internalized every fight scene. He started regressing to needing toilet training again. He put on a smile to mask his hurt. We couldn't go on like this. I would not put my children through the screaming I had heard growing up. Several times, I wished for Ken's death. *I should get my paperwork for my teaching license,* I thought. *I could teach.*

Life with Melo would be easier too.

I had entered the marriage with hopes and dreams of traveling with a charismatic and clever husband. We'd traveled to Colorado and cross-country skied over the tops of pine trees because the snow was so deep it had reached the tips. We'd attended camps with high schoolers and mosquitos in Minnesota. Ken and I had visited other youth leaders in Olympia, New York City, Atlanta, and Winnipeg. I had attended ballet classes in all these cities to master my teaching craft. We'd even visited Didier, a youth minister in the Paris area and a theologian in Germany, for a six-week tour. We'd argued at the top of our lungs in many European cities.

I started making my usual floury mess all over the counter for dinner's homemade pizza, but I lacked the joy I often had while preparing pizza. I hovered where I could not move, where my mind was automatic, and my hands paused on the counter. I took in a deep breath and went out to the backyard to inhale the New England pine. I lit a cigarette. The familiar aroma calmed my disposition and shook me out of paralysis as the nicotine ran through my veins. A few cars passed on the road in front of the house, but I was safely hidden in the backyard. I looked around at the peaceful environment surrounding my gray weathered-cedar home. The quiet was exquisite, broken only an occasional rustling from a critter in the forest.

The two older kids were still in school, and Paul was napping. He and I spent the morning at the "Y" while he climbed through a menagerie of tumbling mats and tunnels. *If I divorced Ken,* I thought, *things would change drastically. I wouldn't be able to stay home and spend precious time alone with Paul.*

I went back into the kitchen and mixed the unbleached flour, salt, yeast, and water. The yeasty dough had to rise for a couple of hours before I could roll it out. The aroma of the sticky dough reminded me of a friend who taught me how to make caramel rolls.

She'd said, "Just hold your finger under the hot water until you can't bear it. Then it's ready for the yeast." I held my hand under the hot water waiting for it to be unbearable. I poured a package of yeast into the almost-too-hot water. The yeasty odor filled the kitchen. For a minute, the aroma made the house a home again.

I thought seriously about leaving or not leaving; I weighed my options. Sitting at my smoking spot on the picnic table, I noticed that the yellow dandelions had sprouted already. *If I leave, where do I go? The monastery, to be a nun? It's a sticky business being a divorced Christian. Would this community scoff at me? Maybe a lawyer could help.*

55

Mom was not available. She stayed to the end in her lavish home. All Mom knew was to stay married no matter what the cost. Divorce would expose the pain that our family of eight was masking. Dad was busy with his girlfriend and had to tell Mom that he was leaving her to get her out of the house.

With the help of Lucy, Mom moved to St. Paul and slept on my sister's couch until she could find a job and a place to live. I thought I could teach French somewhere, but how would I live? Teaching jobs were scarce in Rhode Island, but I knew I'd have to start looking for one.

I wanted to stay home with Paul as I had with the other two children. Paul needed a secure home. All he had heard was yelling.

I went back into the house to make a phone call to get me out of his clutches, to break the mold of me behaving like a Stepford wife.

The phone sat on top of a rolltop desk. The closer I got to the receiver, the harder my heart pounded. Divorce meant breaking up the family and the marriage. My dreams would be gone. I was terrified of the consequences and petrified of the shame. Dread engulfed me. I feared he'd take away what was dearest to me, that he had the power, and I would be an outcast.

"You'll never make it on your own, Mary Beth; no one would hire you," he'd said in a recent argument when I threatened to leave.

I stared at the phone, surrendered, and turned inward to a place of doubt; my shoulders clenched. It had been easier for me to retreat than battle. Calling a lawyer was difficult. I held a double lock on separation of any kind. To stay would mean to submit to an abysmal predicament and shut down. But the shutdown—a tactic I had used before—was no longer tolerable. I picked up the white antique phone receiver from the golden cradle on the laminated rolltop desk. My hand lifted off the "L" section of the yellow pages for Providence. I dialed. The rotary dial clicked repetitively as my finger turned around the smooth numbers, perspiration on my brow.

"Lawyer's office, can I help you?" a female asked.

I cleared my throat. "Yes, I'd like to talk to a lawyer about getting a divorce."

"Please hold."

I looked around the quiet kitchen with its yellow-and-orange flowered wallpaper, and focused on a sunflower while I bit my nails. My thoughts went to a fun first date with Ken when, after a prayer meeting, we had gone to the Pierre capitol grounds, lain on our backs, and watched the northern lights flicker across the night sky. The dew on the grass was pungent. His novel approach to living filled me with joy.

Then, unexpectedly, Ken's quick footsteps came up the driveway. He opened the screen door, quietly closed it, and looked straight at me with his penetrating eyes. Holding my breath, I stared back at him.

"Who are you calling?" he demanded while setting a stack of books on the table.

"A lawyer," I whispered, holding my finger over the button in a stare down. Gently as a child caught with her hand in the cookie jar, I tapped the receiver back in the cradle, releasing all the strength I had mustered to make that call. He ran up to his office two steps at a time, the stairs squeaking under the carpet, and sprinted down as if he knew the power he had over me.

"I forgot something for class." He smiled as if my phone call did not faze him.

He slammed the screen door on his way out while I stood there unable to move. The cornered feeling encased me. I recalled the hitchhiking I'd done in France and Germany. I had taken risks and felt invincible. I said *no* to men and *yes* to adventure. Where had that Mary Beth gone? I wanted that slice of autonomy back. But I told myself, with kids, that life had disappeared for a while.

Later that day, Ken offered to fly me to Pierre to see my family and friends for a week. I enthusiastically agreed, completely unaware that his real plan had been to put me in a treatment facility for a week.

Chapter 12

We returned to Pierre from the KOA campground. To my horror, Ken had arranged for us to stay in a one-bedroom apartment that my sister, Susan, managed. We slept on a foldout with the kids on the bedroom floor, and Paul slept in the closet. Ken started establishing residency in Pierre.

"I'd wipe that look off your face, Mary Beth!" I turned away to hide my tears. He fiddled with the keys. "We are staying in Pierre; can't you get that through your thick skull?" He gave me one nod upward with his chin.

The hot smell of melting asphalt and the bright sun bothered my eyes. The sun beat down on my forehead. My brain scrambled for a logical reason to leave Pierre. A car pulled up in the parking lot and a door slammed. Footsteps faded into the apartment building.

"Ken, I can't live here. I will die if we stay. I left this place a year ago, and I've paid my dues. Thirty years of my life were spent here." I took the car keys out of my pocket and headed for the car.

He jerked my arm.

Bursting into tears, I blubbered. "I miss my house in Rhode Island." I stomped on the asphalt. "Ross said you decided we're staying here." I kicked the cement curb that butted up to the cheap, brown-panel-sided apartment building.

"I've been praying about this, Mary Beth," Ken said between his teeth, his hand still clenching my arm. "God's telling me to settle again in Pierre."

"I've also prayed, Ken, and I'm getting a different response."

He grabbed the back of my neck and looked down at me with protruding eyes and flared nostrils. With his fingers pressed into my throat,

I pulled at his hands but still could not breathe. He let go and slapped me hard across the face.

I let out an uncontrolled moan. "What are you doing?" I asked, my hand on my face.

I ran inside the apartment to the bathroom and locked the door. In the mirror, I saw tiny broken blood vessels that left an imprint of his hand on my cheek.

In a carefully controlled tone, Ken said through the locked door, "Stop talking about Rhode Island, Mary Beth. You'll never see Melo again." He paused and then asked if I was OK.

I was frozen inside. The simple white sink and minimalist shower were all I saw as I sat on the toilet. I covered my face and tried to keep my hands from shaking. It felt like his fingers were still around my throat. I was numb. I pretended that his choking was nothing. Otherwise, I'd be too disgusted with myself and embarrassed about him. I sat inside the bathroom until I heard him talking on the phone. Gabrielle brought Paul in from the swimming pool for his nap. I lifted Paul to my hip. "Come on, Paul. Let's go for a nap. I'll read *Best Word Book Ever*! Your favorite." I managed a smile.

He took my hand, and we cuddled on the sleeping bags in the closet, the only place for him to nap in our makeshift abode. The worn book had pages falling out. The shiny cover was frayed at the corners, exposing the cardboard inside. Paul's giggle became my refuge.

In that dark closet, I read Richard Scarry and looked at the animal drawings. Then Paul's sleepy breathing began. I glanced at the mass of sun-bleached curls that haloed his face, and I could not wait to close my eyes, disappear, and forget about this incredible nightmare for an hour.

Ken took the kids to a leader's home so I could be alone. He knew I had plans with Pam, my sister-in-law. I assumed he would tell no one that he had hit me or choked me. No one had ever confronted him. I tried to imagine him telling his mother what he'd done to me; it was the same behavior his dad had used on her. I hoped he'd tell the proper people and get help. But sadly, I don't know if he ever got honest about his behavior or sought help from a professional. I think he believed that Jesus had healed him or that he was somehow above bad behavior. I was embarrassed that our Christian marriage looked like it did. I didn't like how whiny I'd become. I had to somehow get a grip and move on. When the kids saw and heard us arguing, they must have felt awful. I wondered if he would ever hurt the kids. I had to stuff down my feelings for Melo and consider my dream home a loss. That was the only way this marriage would work. I was not sure if I could do it.

I took out my case of corn-silk powder and stood in front of the mirror. The tiny dots of the broken blood vessels showed through. I smoothed the round powder puff carefully over my cheek. I could still feel the slap. A high collar hid the red marks on my neck.

I thought that I was bad because I didn't know how to fix the marriage.

I watched Pam put her straight hair behind her ear and push her glasses up the bridge of her nose. She handed me a cup of coffee.

"I made cinnamon coffee cake. Would you like some?" She retrieved plates from the white-oak cupboards.

"Yum." I sat at her round oak table following her musings in the kitchen and studying the ways she had decorated her home. She loved wreaths and had a fall one hanging on the door. Her dark, country-style paisley wallpaper was in style then. On top of the desk Ross had built sat a Johnson Brothers white ironstone pitcher. A pillow she had embroidered perched on a Hitchcock chair at the desk. She gave me a napkin and poured me another cup of weak coffee. I wanted to talk about my life, but I was not sure Pam was interested. "So, Pam, how is gymnastics going? Are you enjoying teaching?"

"Yes, it's fun but stressful sometimes."

After she set a dessert plate and fork in front of me, she sat down across from me with the coffee cake and stared at me for an extra second.

"Mary Beth." She leaned forward and gently ran her fingers across my face. "Do you have a rash?"

I gulped down a sob. "I am embarrassed," I said, not knowing how to reveal what I was going to say next.

Pam ignored my comment and waited, handing me a piece of coffee cake. I did not want what I was about to say to be minimized. Mom had endured something similar. I'd heard slaps coming from my parents' bedroom growing up. My bedroom was right next to theirs. No one talked about it, including me. But the screaming and yelling went on practically every night. In the morning, I'd notice Mom's frown. She didn't look at me; she only looked down. She held her coffee cup and sipped as she stared out the window. Certain things were the same, like the fresh-squeezed orange juice in the six small juice glasses. She wore the same tattered robe. There weren't a lot of "I love you"s" or kisses from Mom on those mornings. Dad would smile and leave for work, cleanly shaved, smelling of Old Spice.

I wondered if Pam would blame me and say Ken's anger was justified.

"Ken slapped me," I blurted.

Pam took a big breath and sat back. Her head shook back and forth. Her straight hair fell in front of her glasses as she brought her face up to mine to get a closer look.

"Mary Beth, no one, not even Ken, has the right to hit you."

I looked down, avoiding eye contact, but also wanting to keep the only ally I had. I tried to smile, but I could still see the scenes of thrown pottery, hair dragging, and choking. I let out a long breath that I must have been holding for years.

She squeezed my hand. I focused on the antique coffee grinder with the handle on top behind her.

"Pam, I can't take this much longer. I am more afraid of Ken than ever. He has gone to great lengths to control me. I'm still trying to figure out why he used lies to get me here, to try to put me in an institution, the treatment center. I want him to leave me alone. If I even mention divorce, he will take the kids and maneuver my life with extreme precision."

"I'm sorry, Mary Beth. I don't see him that much. He always seems to know everything. What about couples therapy?"

"Yeah, we went to a counselor before moving to Barrington. We can see the same one, I think."

I never asked nor knew if Pam talked to Ross about Ken slapping me. I never asked Pam why Ross went along with Ken's antics around the treatment center. I still didn't advocate for myself.

Pam's comment and support gave me the beginning of hope that maybe I wasn't all bad. Even though our stay in Pierre had been extended by a few weeks, I was in high spirits when I left Pam's house.

Chapter 13

Back in the dreary apartment, I took an Oreo cookie out of an opened package and dunked it in a glass of milk. There were still boxes on the floor and cans of soup on the counter. Pam and Susan helped us cobble together kitchen dishes and pans for the apartment. I missed my kitchen in Rhode Island, my dishes, the natural light, and the colorful yellow-and-orange sunflower wallpaper. Pam's talk that afternoon made me think. I latched on to her single sentence that no one had the right to hit me. I had finally told someone that he struck me. I felt lighter, but was also still stunned and buoyed by what felt like support. I thought of my mom, who at age fifty-four had started a new life. My thirty-year-old sister, Lucy, who was strong and independent, supported Mom.

Leeanne, a Pierre friend, also lifted me up. But five years earlier, she had been shocked that Ken forbade her to be my friend because of her liberal views and universal theology. She and I had started learning Greek to study the New Testament in a new light. I loved the idea of etymologies and the meanings of words in the original. For example, the word *anthropos* is often translated as "men" when it means "human," both men and women. When the Bible says "God saved all men" in Greek, it means "God saved all men and women." We felt that including women would specifically hit the hearts of women spiritually. I had thought it a noble enterprise.

From my ballet-studio home where I had made Boston cream pies from scratch, I found myself occupying a nothing apartment, eating store-bought cookies from a bag. In the other Pierre home, we'd had a wood-burning stove installed in the open dining and living room area. I used it to bake bread and roasts. I had wanted to "live more with less." The stove had heated our split-level home and cooked our dinners. Ken had helped me arrange the stove and the ballet studio. The home we chose had a wall of windows for my plants. Then I'd purchased my first custom-made woven-beige drapes for the wall of windows. The cathedral ceiling made me feel like a princess. Ken made me feel like a queen in that home . . . a queen with restrictions.

I'd wanted both freedom and to be taken care of by someone. Freedom would bring about new responsibilities. Marriage was supposed to be advantageous over being single. Two versus one: two salaries, two people taking care of the kids, two people helping instead of one. And of course, a loving relationship of give and take.

In France, I had chosen my path: what I wanted to do and where to go every day. I wanted that same autonomy to decide my own daily choices, but within the role of motherhood.

Melo, where are you? Sometimes we took care of each other. And I wanted to be cared for at that moment.

If I told anyone about Ken's physical abuse, he would deny or minimize it. I couldn't breathe thinking about his violence being regarded as nothing. It was huge to me. I did not mention Ken's brutality to Leeanne, nor my sister Lucy. I was an expert at interpreting people. After all, I had learned to watch people as a kid in an angry family. As soon as I walked in a room, I could read the faces and the mood. I understood who would support me. Leeanne would have believed me and told me to get a divorce. But I couldn't find the words to tell her. Unfortunately, I knew that if I told Lucy what Ken had done, she would raise holy hell and tell me to get on a plane with the kids. I was afraid of Ken. I didn't want him to physically keep me in Pierre. He needed me out of Barrington, so he tricked me into flying to Pierre. He'd already taken what I loved away from me: the home I had picked out, my friends there, and Melo. The power Ken exerted over me was the same power I had worshipped when we met. At first, I'd seen him as strong and decisive and loved those things about him. I had hoped his self-confidence would seep into me. Now it was working against me. His control was big in my head, but I still had not tapped my ability to take my own life back. His threats to take the children away from me dominated my thoughts and kept me under his thumb.

We set up a session with the same counselor we had gone to before we moved to Rhode Island. In our weekly marriage counseling, we discussed how we would move forward in a new marriage. Ken tried hard to lift my spirits. We went shopping and bought a classy, white-wool suit for me. I had lost so much weight I needed new clothes. Plus, my other clothes were still out east.

He was determined to find a job in Pierre. I was realizing that we really might stay there. It was September, and the kids had started school at the elementary school. The day it snowed in September, I sat in front of the window and cried. I couldn't believe the East Coast was gradually fading from my life. Just like when I arranged my year in France, I again wanted out of Pierre.

I sat in our counselor's makeshift office. She began with the usual: "How are we doing this week?" She turned to both of us. Boxes were piled around her desk. "Mary Beth? What's going on?" I looked down at my chair, one of many therapy chairs I had sat in during the marriage. Her office looked temporary, as did my marriage.

"I can't do this anymore." My hands hid my eyes.

Ken snorted. "Can't do what?"

"Pretend that I can live in Pierre." I considered the stack of boxes behind her desk. "Because I can't."

"We're not going back to Rhode Island!" Ken warned with a pointed finger. "We're staying here." He folded his arms.

No one said anything for a minute. The silence gave me time to slow my breathing down. I took a deep breath. "Then I want to talk about divorce."

Ken at once scraped the chair back, stood up, and said he had to make a phone call.

He was aghast that I had said the forbidden word. My East Coast dream was lost, and staying in Pierre was worse than being married. I refused to stay in Pierre and wither.

The counselor and I sat looking at each other, dumbfounded. She wrote something down on a notepad. I closed my eyes, knowing Ken was not going to agree to a divorce. Maybe he was planning to go back to Rhode Island. Maybe my bold statement scared him. We heard his mumbling in the hallway. Then he appeared in the open doorway with a phone in his hand and pulled the black coiled line.

"He wants to talk to you."

"Who?"

"Your dad."

"What? Did you call him? We're in a counseling session." I felt brave with the counselor there. "No, I'm not talking to him."

I did not realize, at that time, the distances Ken went to control me. This call to my dad was similar to what he'd done when I was depressed after learning about his affair with Pauline. That first year of marriage, Ken had urged my dad to come over to our apartment. Dad had told me that if I got pregnant and had a baby, things would change, and my marriage would be better.

I did not want to listen to my dad about my broken marriage. He had failed at his own miserably. I pressed my heels into the ground. I still felt utterly betrayed by my dad's alliance with Ken.

"Why don't you come back and finish this session, Ken?" the counselor asked with wide eyes and a controlled voice.

Physically, socially, spiritually, and emotionally, I had left Pierre a year earlier.

I sat up straighter and, in a louder voice, said, "I have a suggestion."

"Yes, Mary Beth?" The counselor encouraged me as she leaned forward.

Ken stopped picking the skin on his thumb and turned his head, his gaze fixed on me.

"I cannot stay in Pierre . . ." I hesitated. "And if I can't have Barrington, at least Minneapolis would give me breathing room." I thought Ken might take up my offer.

Chapter 14

"I'll look at houses in Minneapolis." He glanced at me as he stood.

I turned away and twisted my gold wedding ring with an embedded silver cross that was supposed to reminded us that Jesus was at the center of our marriage. It now had a tiny diamond too. Someone told me the ring looked like it was from a religious order. I could not muster an agreement to Ken's house-hunting decision. A home was critical to me because I had more sovereignty in that space. In my mind, the ballet studio house was created for me, as was the Barrington colonial. I ruled there. I didn't care anymore which Minneapolis house I lived in, but I knew for sure that I didn't want to reside in Pierre. This was a baby step on my part. In the counseling office, I began to let go of the imprint, the branding that Pierre had stamped on my life. The many eyes I felt were on me in Pierre diminished with the thought of anonymity in Minneapolis.

The house in Barrington, Rhode Island, still had not sold, but my holdout to move back to the East Coast faded, which sickened me. Even though the house had not sold, I mourned the inevitability that it soon would be lost.

We didn't talk about finances. Ken gave me money for groceries; I was not privy to our family budget, just like my mom had not been. She got a monthly stipend from Dad. How much money had we lost by keeping the Rhode Island house empty for five months? Did Ken pay that mortgage, or did he foreclose? And how did he pay for the apartment in Pierre? Did he borrow money or spend his pension? Supposedly we had been on a budget all these twelve years of marriage. Where did he get this money to pay for this new mortgage in Minneapolis? I didn't ask him these questions. I was in captive mode. I didn't feel I had a right. I worried that questions might erupt a volcano, so we communicated nothing between us. My gut spun.

When our house in Rhode Island sold, Ken found a house on Grand Avenue in Minneapolis. Both our names were on the title. But somehow, only he was the one to be at the closing in Rhode Island. There was no way he would chance me going back to Barrington. I knew that much. I never knew what happened to the money from the sale of the colonial house. I didn't inquire.

"I think you'll like it, Mary Beth." He sounded upbeat and hopeful.

It happened fast. My grieving continued for the home out east. Somehow, I felt that all these possessions, myself, and the kids were Ken's chattels.

The kids and I pulled up to the white house on a south Minneapolis corner. It looked like a small cottage, but it was cute. Ken was standing in the doorway with a big smile. The kids ran into his arms.

I slowly walked up and pulled him aside.

"What are we going to do with all our stuff in Rhode Island? I haven't even seen it for five months!"

"I'll bring it here by U-Haul after the closing."

"This house is half the size of the Barrington house. It's crap!" I walked through to the kitchen and glanced at a built-in table breakfast booth. It was obvious Ken had tried his hardest to get a house I might like, but I refused to surrender or let him know that I liked it even a little. The Minneapolis compromise had put Ken in an energetic frenzy to save our marriage. I, on the other hand, felt like giving up. The knot in my throat rose until I almost started to cry.

His smile dissolved at my comment. The kids ran through the house, then scampered outside. "What?" he blasted. "I'm bringing everything of yours and mine back here to Minneapolis! Mary Beth, you must get a grip on this. You need to grow up, for heaven's sake. We are here in Minneapolis starting a new life, and hopefully, a new marriage. Look at your finger. I had the jeweler insert that diamond in your wedding ring as a symbol of our new start." I looked at my left ring finger. I had just gone along with his ideas for a renewed marriage and dropped my opinion of diamonds. I had protested diamonds in favor of something different when we married in 1972 because of the conditions under which they were mined.

Ken started to raise his voice. Sweating, I ran upstairs, felt vomit in my throat, and stood at the top of the steps. The East Coast and Melo were gone forever.

"I'm still talking to you!" He yelled as he followed me up the stairs.

"Turn around and look at me when I'm talking to you!" His voice echoed in the empty house, and his breath smelled like mint when he put his face in mine.

"I'm done," I squeaked and backed up.

"Done what?" He started for me, leaning forward and going for my arm with his hands.

"Done talking." I kept trying to move away from him.

"I'm not! Come 'ere!"

I slammed the bathroom door behind me. I locked it, then knelt in front of the toilet and threw up. There was no toilet paper in the tiny empty bathroom, so I wiped my drool with my sleeve. Leaning against the toilet, I sat still on the floor.

Even though I had made baby steps in declaring Minneapolis as a compromise, escaping the dark nightmare of entrapment still seemed impossible. My marriage needed undoing.

Reagan had just won the November presidential race.

The U-Haul Ken had packed with our belongings in Rhode Island pulled up. He'd left behind many things that I cherished. I picked up the dolly with drawers full of Chris's play clothes. His jeans looked too small for him. It had been five months. The dolly pushed my spirits even lower. As I moved things into the small white house, I saw all that I'd loved in Rhode Island dissolve. Ken had tried his best when he picked out a small gabled house with a screened-in porch and a balcony on top. I could see he'd tried to pick the style he knew I cherished. But the damage had been done. I could not visualize the new life he was hoping for. I kept my armor on to protect myself from trusting him. At least the Minneapolis air was breathable, and my mother and sister lived there.

The three kids were fighting. I dumped the drawers in front of Ken.

"Well," he said. "You sure have a lot of energy." He smiled and tried to look into my eyes. I gave him nothing, and I needed space from him.

I volunteered to blow insulation into the attic the next day. I relished the retreat. It was a refuge and a sanctuary for me. I craved a safe house and insulation from Ken.

My hands held the hose, and I stared at the clumps of gray particles that covered the floor. The particles made a pile in one corner of the attic. This was going to be a long hiatus from my family downstairs. Ken fed the insulation into the hose. My tears flowed into my mask. The light from the attic vent made bright stripes on the floor.

What message was I sending to my children? That women and mothers have no power to reach for what they want. That men dominate and make the rules.

I lifted my mask and breathed in the musty scent of the enclosed attic. My shoes disappeared into the gray blanket of insulation.

Separating myself from the changes that I felt I had no control over, my thoughts went to her. I wondered where Melo was at that moment. Her expressions I loved were disappearing in my head. What was she doing right then in her dorm? In that space where the scent of mixed crispness permeated the long hallway. Even Chris stopped calling out her name.

Standing in the slanted attic, holding the noisy hose, I disappeared. The gray specks of loose insulation vanished into the far corners of the tiny dark attic. It seemed like the attic never filled up. It just stayed the same, stagnant as my life was. I held the hose, and my pain did not change. Yet, I savored every minute of the attic buffer.

I didn't know how I was going to do this next stage of my life. Then, like a robot, I exited the attic sanctuary down to the house to organize our belongings in a new home in Minneapolis.

Chapter 15

"Hi, Debra! Can you believe it! Ken picked out a house only three blocks away from you!" We hugged.

A longtime friend and feminist, she gave me an incredulous stare as we stood in front of her house. "You didn't at least help choose your own home, Mary Beth?"

I waved off her comment with a nervous laugh. "I'm working on it, Debra." I touched my neck. "I was in a trance back in Pierre."

"What do you mean?"

"We almost stayed there with all the people he's influenced, including my own family." With my chin up and a knowing grin, I said, "It was my idea to come to Minneapolis."

With a booming laugh, she said, "And I'm glad you did."

The long blond hair she'd had since high school had been cut shorter, just beneath her chin. We laughed at our coup. In high school, we'd lived three blocks apart, and here we were in Minneapolis still three blocks apart.

We chose the Minnehaha Parkway as a jogging route. Hip alongside hip, we started our jog under tunneled tree-lined paths beside an often-bubbling creek.

"What happened, Mary Beth? Tell me why you are here and not in Rhode Island?"

Starting at the beginning was difficult. She listened in horror and offered continual support, lifting me from my nightmare. Even though I knew she'd disliked Ken from the first day she met him, she did not belittle him. We continued in silence under I-35W. The whooshing of cars drowned out the sound of our shoes patting the asphalt trail.

"I do have to say, Mary Beth, that I couldn't stand the way he manipulated our little sisters to join his club. His one-liners seemed phony. I just kept my mouth shut around you when you two got together."

I stopped and put my hands on my knees. I wasn't used to jogging. "Debra, my heart is broken, and my children are in distress. Ken and I are hanging on by a thin hair," I said while gulping for air.

Over the next few months, she listened to the story of my previous twelve years with Ken. I cried while I ran. Verbalizing my feelings to a friend seemed to help me heal and see things more clearly. We eventually ran a few 10-Ks together.

On one of the Bonne Bell races, Ken stood at the finish line and took pictures. In the sea of mostly women, I noticed tears in his eyes as he brought the camera down from his face. I had done my best to come in just over an hour. What a sad situation we both were in. He wanted into my life, and all I felt was entrapment.

"I'm at a loss for words, Mary Beth," Debra said. "You seemed stronger in high school. Now, this guy tells you what to do and where to live."

I began to realize I needed to start the process of teaching French. She said she would show me around the University of Minnesota so I could get my license updated.

I smiled cautiously. She reminded me of Melo. Debra knew what to do and did not need a man to show her.

Ken confronted me as I came in sweaty and sat on the front steps to smoke. "Why don't you call Sara instead of Debra?" he asked through the screen door. "Besides, aren't Debra's politics a bit leftist?"

"Back off, Ken," I snapped at him. "You have your friends here, and I have mine!" Just having a listener like Debra gave me the confidence to speak a bit more of my mind. I was not going to let him dictate who my friends were anymore.

We both must have thought of Melo at that moment, because he added, "I check the phone bills, you know."

My back was to him, so I smiled to myself just thinking about her. I walked into the smaller living room, which did not hold all my Rhode Island furniture. The piano, couch, and wingback chairs lined the walls, my desk up next to the front door. Our light-blue woven-rag rug was missing, along with my ballet mirrors. Paul sat on the floor watching *Mr. Rogers' Neighborhood* on TV. I walked past him into the dining room, where the ladderback chairs stood stiffly at attention around the paper-strewn table-top. The light from the south sunroom warmed the dining room.

That weekend, Ken arranged a dinner with Sara and her husband, Bill. I had renewed a friendship with Sara, a friend of ours from the youth ministry. Bill, a youth minister in Minneapolis, was attractive in many ways. He was a loving husband and an accomplished guitar player. He and Sara both laughed often. They had a huge, beautiful home with built-in buffets and dark woodwork on Diamond Lake Road. I lusted after it. She had that pointy turned-up nose that I'd always wanted. She had a sense of freedom that I wanted. Her humor often lifted my spirits. At the weekend dinner, we played charades in the oak-trimmed family room.

"TV shows!" I yelled as she made a big square with her hand, then quick-ly held up four fingers. Her short hair framed her beautiful, sculpted face.

"Four words!" She stuck out her front teeth and bounced and walked with her wavy hands behind her butt. I rolled in laughter.

"Beaver! *Leave It to Beaver*!"

"Yes!"

She made me laugh until I practically wet my pants. Playing a game with a not-so-serious friend lifted me out of the darkness for a time. I still was not eating much, but laughing helped me eat more and forget the pain. I chose friends based on their personalities and what I lacked in comparison. Their hilarity displayed their ease. I was drawn to her joy and sense of hu-mor, and I hoped to learn to be fortunate like her. I saw and longed for her happiness and her status, but I only knew how to be a "good girl." Ken did not bring up any of our problems as far as I knew.

One evening, after dinner, Sara and Bill showed up unannounced ac-companied by a man I did not know. The pot-roast, carrot, and potato din-ner was still on the table beside dirty dishes. They stood at my door smiling.

"This is a friend of ours from church," Sara said, laying a hand over her heart. "He's one of the pastors."

"I'll put the kids to bed, Mary Beth. You can pour them some coffee." Ken went upstairs. I had begun waking up internally to the many ways he ordered me around, but externally, I was still the dutiful wife.

I was delighted and excited to see Sara and Bill. The timing was perfect because I wanted to laugh like I usually did with Sara. We sat very quietly and stiffly around our living room.

The stranger wore a dark suit with no tie and sat on the edge of my wingback chair with his worn black-leather Bible on his lap. The edges of the pages were shiny gold. His neatly combed brown hair was parted on one side, and his face was clean shaven. He did not say much. He seemed to be about our age.

Ken came down quietly with a finger over his lips, as though he always put the kids to bed. The guests seemed to be waiting for Ken to sit down and join us. There was little small talk.

"Mary Beth," the preacher began with a pasted-on smile. He cleared his throat. "You have—or should I say you *had*—this friend, Melo, back in Rhode Island?"

I shot Sara a glance. She bounced her knee and gave me no eye contact.

He continued without a pause. "Have you heard of Jezebel?" He looked directly at me.

I stiffened. Only Ken's look bored through me.

"She is from Satan, pure evil, and breaks up marriages. We believe"—he looked around the room—"that Melo is possessed by the evil spirit Jezebel."

My jaw opened; I was speechless. For a second, I wanted to hide. I could not think straight. I looked down in front of Sara and her husband. The coffee tasted bitter. I looked across the living room and saw my Sara, her foot rocking and making a squeaking sound. They were the folks I trusted and looked up to. My chest tightened with a huge lump in my gut. Ken was now avoiding my eyes.

"What Bible verses did you use to justify your actions with Melo?"

After scanning each face in the room, I ordered myself to calm down. Then, without hesitation, I quoted, "Mark 12:30–31. Love the Lord your God with all your heart, mind, body, and soul, and love your neighbor as yourself.'"

The preacher turned away from me and toward Sara and her husband, hugging his Bible to his chest and signaling with his eyes. Then he used the Bible as his pointer.

"You think about what I just said, Mary Beth. This is serious stuff."

"I don't know you at all. But Sara–" I fought back tears and curled my lips inward.

Sara and her husband stood. Bill tucked in his shirt with his big smile that I adored. Sara had a half smile like she was going to tell a joke but then stopped and cleared her throat with her fist up to her mouth.

Ken and I stood with them. They left as abruptly as they'd come. Ken went into the kitchen and made his usual late-night snack of vanilla ice cream with milk poured on top.

In silence, I did the dishes, questions swirling in my head. Had he sought her out and told them whatever he wanted? Why did she believe him before coming to me? This was an intervention all over again. Wherever we went, he made me look like shit. *What does he want?* I wondered. *A little Christian wife who adores him? Well, buddy, that wife is long gone.*

Ken settled alone in the living room with his bowl of ice cream. After putting the dishes away, I stood at the bottom of the stairs. He slowly took a bite, making sure he added some milk to the spoon. Then, without hurrying, he brought a cloth napkin up to his mustache.

"Did you set this up, Ken?" He took another spoonful and set it in the dish, then put the dish on the end table. He carefully wiped his mouth again. I stood in the dark room as the end-table lamp lit him up like an MC at a performance.

"Yes, I did."

"Ken." I shook my head. "Really?" I raised my voice. "You're telling lies about me! Again! Everywhere we go!" I felt cornered like a stray dog at the end of an alley. Ken, the dog catcher, was coming toward me. He knew I adored Sara. He'd used her as bait.

After finishing another bite, he swallowed, "I have to protect you from demons, Mary Beth. You can't protect yourself."

"I need protection from you!" I countered.

Chapter 16

At the end of the next marriage-counseling session, I screamed in his face, "I have nothing else to lose!"

Ken stared at me, took in a breath, and for once had no comeback. He shifted in his seat. "What can I do to make this marriage work?" Sweat beads formed on his brow. We all sat in silence.

Finally, with composure, I announced, "I'm going to my Adult Children of Alcoholics group this week. I will let you both know what I am going to do at our next session."

My Thursday night ACA meeting met in the basement of the Walker United Methodist Church. It was an expansive lunchroom, and the tables had been moved to one side. I had been going weekly since we moved to Minneapolis. The people I met were about my age. They were artistic and tried things I hadn't tried yet. They introduced me to the Mayday Parade, camping, biking, and CDs (which had just come out). People were tossing their cassette tapes. I'd sought out this ACA group because the folks I met there listened and asked pertinent questions that hit home. We divided ourselves into small groups of five or six and sat on chairs in a circle. Maybe seventy people came in total. My group knew I was struggling in a violent marriage.

"Mary Beth, tell us what you want. What do you need?"

It felt new and provocative to be asked those questions. I tingled just thinking about my answer. It took a while, but I started visualizing my needs. I was reading Melody Beattie's book *Codependent No More*, and it was helping me to see and understand myself better. I was a codependent person in a codependent relationship, but I had the right to be happy. I shared with them about my marriage and got support for sticking up for myself. Hoping for a ceasefire, I began crafting a list of needs.

When I came home from the meeting, Ken started right in, his voice thundering. "Who are these people you meet with anyway? Are they Christians? I don't even know them!"

"Back off, Ken!" Paul was sitting halfway down the stairs, listening and peeking through the banister.

"Mommy, I'm sad. You and Daddy are fighting." He put his head in his hands, mimicking me.

"I'm sorry, honey." I stood up and reached toward him, running my fingers through his sweaty blond curls. "We'll stop now." I lifted him onto my lap and paused to look at Ken. "See, there's no more fighting."

Ken joined me on the stairs beside Paul. "Hey, little buddy, Mommy and I don't want to keep arguing. We'll work on it." He turned to me. "Right, Mommy?"

I began to see that our charade wasn't working with the kids.

"Are you going back to Rhode Island?" Paul's tiny voice was filled with unpretentious questions.

"No, honey." My eyes welled up again. "Come on, let's get back to bed." I took his hand and started up the stairs.

The next morning, Gabrielle descended, frowning, her disheveled chestnut hair on her face.

"What's the matter, honey?" I scooped oatmeal with raisins into a bowl.

She moped and slouched in the table booth. "Are you and Dad going to get a divorce?" She gazed at me while she poured milk on her oatmeal, adding a teaspoon of brown sugar.

I kept my back turned, trying to avoid having to answer.

"You're always yelling, and it hurts my heart." Her voice cracked as she continued to hold her spoon up in the air. I rushed over to her, slid in next to her, and put my arms around her small nine-year-old body. My whole being was crushed; she should not have had to process our problems.

"Things are rough between Daddy and me, Gabrielle, but we're trying to work it out." My fingers wrapped a string of her hair around her ear. "I'm sorry you have to hear our screaming at each other." I planted a kiss on the top of her head.

"I'm scared that—that someone will go away. Is this Melo's fault?"

I straightened up, angry. "No, not at all." I turned off the stove.

"Dad doesn't like her," she said. I did not respond.

"Dad doesn't like who?" Chris quipped with a smile as he bounced down the stairs, his straight bangs lined up above the eyebrows of his still-round face.

"Melo," volunteered Gabrielle.

"You like her, right, Mom?" he said with a louder tone and arched eyebrows.

"Yes, I do." I set down a bowl for him across from Gabrielle.

"Melo, Melo," Chris chanted, "Mom likes Melo!" just as Ken walked in the door.

On Friday, when I walked into the subdued room of our counseling session, my steps were a bit lighter. Ken had set up the session with a Christian guy from Bethel College. The half-basement room had windows at ground level. I had spent hours contemplating the question *what do I need?* I concluded that because I had lost everything—my home in Rhode Island, Melo, my integrity—I would go straight to my heart's desires to answer that question. I carefully wrote out my prayer for integrity and the ability to get back on my feet. I had nothing to lose.

My hands and voice were shaking as I unfolded my wrinkled handwritten list of the things I needed if I was going to continue in the marriage. The counselor made Ken listen without interrupting.

1. *I want Ken to write an apology to Melo.*

2. *I want Ken to write an apology to several people at the college in Rhode Island, including the president and vice president of the college. These folks were my friends; Ken blasted my reputation with them, and I need him to repair the damage he'd done.*

3. *I want to go and visit the Christian college in Rhode Island and go to Melo's graduation.*

4. *I want Melo to come and visit our family in Minneapolis, so Ken can right the wrongs with the children and Melo.*

5. *Finally, I want Ken and me to focus on my career for the next ten years. If it meant moving to where I can get a job, then so be it.*

I was met with total silence. My heart pounded. It felt like a huge rock had been lifted. Unknowingly, I'd left out another item from the list: an apology to myself.

Ken nodded with a sigh. He looked out the window, picking at his thumb in silence.

Chapter 17

I was nervous; I had not seen Melo in over a year. But I still thought of her daily and prayed for her. I arrived at Logan Airport. My heart pounded and my hands shook. The first glimpse of her was glorious. Her hair was cut differently; the perm had grown out. She approached me. She had Benjamin, her teddy bear, nestled under her arm. He matched her smooth tan oxfords. We hugged for a long time. I inhaled her loamy scent. We smiled at each other and held hands while she drove. Sometimes the depth of the passion I felt for her surprised me.

"What do we do first?" We both giggled like two playmates who had the whole afternoon with no parents.

Melo drove me to her dorm. The crisp smell of the hallway was familiar. She still had up pictures of my lookalike, Pat Benatar. She was wound up, moving in quick steps, her long eyelashes lowered in timidity. A *Welcome Mary Beth!* banner hung across her room from the window to the corner.

"I cleaned all day yesterday and made these for you." She handed me several soft macramé bracelets. "So, Ken was fine with you coming?" She sat down on a beanbag chair, and I leaned back on my elbows on her bed. If our age difference was an issue, I ignored it.

"Yes, I wrote five conditions for me to stay married, and for once he's taking me seriously. At least I think he is."

"I'm happy for you, Mary Beth. Maybe this will work out."

Melo was full of energy, smiling broadly.

"Let's just have fun this weekend." It felt like I was in another body, a free, flowing one. "Oh, Melo, here's a card made by Chris. He said, 'Give it to her right away.'"

She jumped up. "Let me see. Is that me and him playing hacky sack?" she asked with a laugh.

I nodded, taking a big breath. I asked her if she had received an apology from Ken. She said no.

After the graduation ceremony, Melo showed me the used motorcycle she'd bought. She grabbed a backpack, and we went motorcycling to my favorite place: Newport, out past the harbor of sailboats that reminded me of France. We walked around the point on the cliff, past the famous colonial houses, sometimes shyly holding hands. She chose a patch of grass to have lunch.

"Let's eat right here." Out of her backpack appeared a chocolate bar, tuna sandwiches, chips, and two cherry Cokes. "Can you believe we're here together, along the ocean?"

Being together felt strange for me. I had never gone from point A to point B without checking in with someone, Mom or Ken. At age thirty-five, this was a big taste of freedom!

We motorbiked back to Newport. The power of the motor beneath me and my arms around her electrified the moment. I stuck my face into the back of her neck to the fresh, clean smell of her T-shirt and skin. As we leaned in unison around a corner, my body held tight to hers. I was in heaven! We shared a strawberry tart from the French bakery, biked across the suspension bridge, and laughed all afternoon.

I loved sitting behind her because I could hold on tight for prolonged periods. Eventually, I moved my hand up inside her shirt to touch her breast. I noticed she was braless. My skin to her intimate skin gave me a heated rush. It was electrifying. I could feel her inhale and let it out with a side glance. She smiled slightly. The roar of the motorbike drowned out any conversation.

We stopped back at the dorm.

"So, I touched your breast." I looked at her to see her reaction and see if it was OK.

"I know," she said. "The feelings I have for you scare me."

I took her hand and hugged her body close to mine.

My love for her was very intense; I did not understand it completely. I tried hard to put sexual thoughts behind me, but I could not deny that I had them. My thoughts turned to Ken and the kids at home. I had to reconcile these two worlds—Melo, and my family. I wondered if I'd intentionally lit a fuse to a bomb that I wanted to go off. I knew that in my conflicted state, I didn't have the wherewithal to toss the grenade. I felt the answer would come when they converged later that summer.

"Thank you, Melo, for all my wishes coming true. Now we can plan your trip to Minneapolis."

Ken picked me up at the airport; he was happy to see me, but quiet too. He waited for me to start up the conversation. I told him about the fun things we'd done and the folks he knew who sent greetings. I left out the hugs, holding hands, and private love words. He pushed nothing, but he did ask when Melo was coming for her visit.

"In two months."

Chapter 18

Melo arrived with smiles and gifts. She had already started a job in Rhode Island before arriving at our home. Again, at the airport, we hugged for a long embrace. I was so nervous and distracted that I missed the exit two times coming home. I was confident that she loved me no matter where I lived and no matter how many times I said we could or couldn't see each other. We both romanticized our relationship as being blessed by God.

She talked about a supervisor at her job; it sounded like she had feelings for another woman like the feelings she expressed for me. I tucked that fear into the back of my mind.

Ken was nervous too. He greeted her with a hug and made efforts to ask questions about her job and life in Rhode Island. I was proud of the positive gestures he was making toward Melo. I was hopeful that everything would turn out. I wanted him happy, and I wanted it all.

After unpacking, Melo played with the kids, especially Chris. We all sat on the couch in the sunroom next to the dining room and watched a VHS video of *The NeverEnding Story* while eating popcorn and giggling. Standing in the sunroom doorway, Ken scrutinized us with a furrowed brow. "Do you have to sit so close together, Mary Beth?"

"Ken, we're fine. There is only one couch here. Why don't you get a chair and come sit with us?" I jiggled closer to Melo; I felt her muscular legs next to mine. "Or we can scooch over, and you join us."

He turned and walked away without a word.

I did not want to change what I did around Melo. I bounced between the fairy tale that we could all be together in harmony and the reality that things might get ugly. I already had gone down deep into the depths of rage toward Ken and had seen his fury. But I didn't have a plan; I wanted to see if it could work with Melo around us. Or maybe I wanted him to hurt like I had been hurt. I justified sitting close to her in my mind and refused to accommodate Ken. If he was upset, too bad.

We all loaded up inner tubes, beach balls, and Frisbees, piled in the car, and drove the two miles to Lake Harriet. The kids squealed and shouted as they played in the sand and splashed in the lake. Chris wanted me to show him how to swim. Ken sat with his sunglasses and a shirt on, surveying us like a lifeguard, his arms resting on his knees. I was not going to let his surveillance ruin our time.

After teaching Chris to float, Melo and I paddled the inner-tube boat out to the middle of the lake. We were facing each other with our knees touching and legs dangling over the inner tube. Away from inspecting eyes, I quickly stuck my bare wet foot into Melo's swim top, much to her surprise.

Ken rowed with Paul from the shore to where we were. Ken frowned as he circled our inner tube and bellowed that it was time to leave.

After a chicken dinner and layered banana-split ice-cream dessert, Melo and I put the kids to bed. Ken poked his head inside the bedroom. Melo, Gabrielle, and I were talking about the day. He expressed his concern over the two of us lying with Gabrielle on her bed. He ran his hand through his curly blond hair in frustration.

"We are touching each other because we are lying close to each other, not because we're doing something wrong, Ken! Come on! Back off!" All my earlier suppressed anger started spilling out in these words to Ken.

He stayed there staring. His lips formed a tight line under the broom-like mustache.

Melo's presence gave me strength. We pushed it to the limits. I no longer tried to hide my feelings for Melo nor really saw myself as married to this man. I just needed more time to gather my internal forces and stop gas-lighting Ken. I was at the brink of ending my marriage and finding a way for Melo and me to be together. I was strong enough to try to strike out on my own but not yet strong enough to admit the extent of my feelings for Melo. It did not cross my mind how different things would have been if Melo had been a male friend. I would not ask Ken to accept my "friend-ship" with a male friend. The boundaries would be obvious to me. I let this female friendship stay close to my heart because I wanted it and could justify a friendship with a woman. Each day she stayed, I moved closer to her and further from any desire to keep my marriage going.

Melo and I went to my Adult Children of Alcoholics meeting that evening.

"Do you have to go?" Ken asked after we finished the dishes.

It was good to be alone together because things were near to boiling over with Ken. After the meeting, I thought intensely about stopping in a secluded area. Eventually, I turned off onto a quiet unlit street by Lake Harriet. When I drew her close and looked down at her eyes, they shone vividly through her long lashes. I thought of her soft lips on mine and kissed her. My tongue searched around the inside of her mouth. With my eyes closed, I held her close. Her breath increased in arousal. Mine did too. I wanted the moment to last forever. *What am I doing? I am making out with her—like a teenager in high school!* I thought. *I am doing exactly what Ken feared most.* I felt shame at lying to Ken in front of the kids. I felt guilty.

"Melo, I'm crossing boundaries, here."

She held her breath, then let it out. "I know." And lowered her gaze.

The next day, Ken started screaming at the bottom of the stairs.

"I am sick and tired of the way you and Melo act around each other." He kicked the stairs.

My fingers pawed my hair as I sat down on the flight of steps. I couldn't find the right words. "Ken, we are acting normal. We are close. We have no agenda." I suppressed the image of us kissing in the car the previous night. "We love each other." I had denied my love and desire for Melo for so long, even while I explored my sexuality with her. I still looked for straws to grasp to keep the good-wife smokescreen.

His eyes bugged out. He exhaled fast and did an about-face toward the door. He paced in the living room while Melo watched silently from the kitchen booth.

With a tightness in my chest, I continued restraining my voice. "Melo and I are going nowhere." I followed him around the living room, stuffing my shaking hands in my jeans pockets. "Two friends can hold hands, kiss, and hug." Feeling fearless, my denial kicked in. "You remember in Europe? Women held hands and walked down the street? You're overreacting."

He slammed the coffee table with his fist and turned to Melo with a pointed finger. "You have no business being here." She blinked back tears.

"Ken, remember, this is part of our agreement, my conditions for you know what." I gestured toward the kids with my head, avoiding the "D" word. "You agreed to Melo's visit." My voice rose uncontrollably. I knew I was fooling myself. Ken had a right to be angry concerning my behavior with Melo. If he'd had a woman he wanted to keep by his side, as I did with Melo, I would have become incredibly angry. It crushed me that the kids were hearing all this. They were in pain. I had to decide.

Living with Ken and denying my sexual feelings for Melo was not working. I pulled him aside and whispered, "Besides, you and Pauline held hands and kissed. And what else do I not know that you haven't revealed?" Now my face jutted into his space. "What have you lied to me about?"

And our children—*Oh Jesus, help me!* I prayed.

Ignoring my question, he closed his eyes and inhaled. "I take it back. This arrangement with Melo here isn't working for me, and now I'm late for my meeting." He picked up his leather briefcase, unbuckled it, and put his Bible inside. The door slammed as he left.

Melo pulled me aside from the stunned children. "Mare, look." She pulled out a wad of cash. "Let's get out of here and go to an amusement park."

Chapter 19

We escaped to Valleyfair. The kids' faces looked shell shocked in the rear-view mirror for the entirety of the quiet forty-five-minute ride.

Melo turned to face the kids. "Hey, kids, we're going to have fun at Valleyfair! Who wants to have fun?" No one answered.

Ken and my screaming at each other were still ringing in my ears. We had stopped hiding our arguments long ago. Maybe their ears were also ringing.

When we got out in the sea of cars at the huge Valleyfair parking lot, Chris looked at the tallest roller coaster and said with a big smile, "That's what I'm going to do!"

"No, Chris, that's for grown-ups," I said as I picked up Paul and put him on my hip.

Chris jumped out and accidentally nicked the car parked next to us.

"Oh, honey, look what you did." I frowned and pointed to the dent. I sat Paul down.

Chris looked up at me, puffed up his chest, and slammed the car door another three times into the same car as hard as he could, making the dent larger. Tears streamed down his reddened face.

I grabbed his arm, pulled him up in the air, and spanked his butt as hard as I could. My hand hit his bottom repeatedly. He screamed and tried to get away.

I was out of control.

Gabrielle's tears welled up, and Paul watched wide-eyed. Melo took a few steps backward. Her jaw dropped.

When I tried to hold Chris's hand, he recoiled. We left the parking lot with a newly dented car next to ours and no offer to take responsibility on my part. The sparkling neon lights and carnival sounds awaited us. We were silent.

We all relaxed a bit at the amusement park; the kids had fun. The distraction of the rides and cotton candy worked for a while. Something had to be done—I could not keep up with the anger in our home. I couldn't have it all and make everyone happy. I couldn't hit my child again. I had to end this marriage for the last time. I let go of the idea of a fairy tale and living happily ever after.

When we came back from the amusement park, Ken was pacing.

"Melo!" he shouted. "Get out of my house!"

She started crying and left through the front door. I felt protective of her but did nothing. After we screamed at each other for another twenty minutes, I left the house too, looking up and down the street for Melo. I landed at Debra's house, where I felt safe. But I returned home for fear that Ken would accuse me of abandonment.

That night was the first real step toward ending our twelve years of marriage. I said goodbye to Debra and Karl and their peaceful home and proceeded back to my stormy house.

When I returned, the door was locked. Ken's brother opened the door just a crack like I was the criminal. I found Melo down the street on the steps of a mortuary, called the police so I could get back in the house, and went inside.

She slept on the couch. I took her to the airport the next day. I apologized and told her that our love was still as strong as the yellow star in Orion. She was mostly tearful.

I decided that enough was enough. Our marriage was doing damage to the children. I could see that. I had hit my breaking point while spanking Chris. I'd become the violent one with the kids, not Ken. My children were no longer going to witness our tragic marriage. They were not going to learn from their parents how to destroy each other anymore. Suddenly, I knew that I would do everything in my power to heal them and myself.

Chapter 20

After Melo left, the kids started school. Our marriage was in tatters. It was raining. The earthy smell of the water entering the soil permeated the room through the open windows. Ken was about to return to work. He just stood in the entryway, looking at me and biting the inside of his cheek.

He looked at the stack on the desk by the front door. "Why are you applying to schools? They're never going to hire you."

"Have you been mailing my job applications?"

He did not answer, his hand resting on the door frame.

"You're ignoring my needs, Ken. Remember!" I pointed to myself. "My career?" He said nothing. I sat down on the bottom step of the staircase.

"Everything I do, Mary Beth, is for you and our happiness." He paced.

"Our happiness?! Our?! You mean everything you do is for *your* happiness! You do not get it, Ken. Where is the encouragement for a teaching position?" I stood eye to eye with him.

"Teaching? You will never be able to get a job, much less support us on a teaching salary. You don't have it in you. You are too dependent on me."

"I'm divorcing you," I screamed.

"Divorce is not an option," he yelled, coming at me.

Crack was the rock-hard sound of him slapping me on the face. My eyes and cheeks felt hot. I wanted "us" to end at all costs.

"We're done! You can't hit me anymore or hurt me or put me naked on that fucking pedestal any longer!" My eyes felt like they were popping out of my head. Hair in my face, I twisted it into a ponytail. Feeling empowered and strong, I was not going to let him hurt me anymore.

He said he was sorry, that he wouldn't do it again. He sat with his head in his hands and cried, knowing this was the last straw. I didn't trust his words anymore. He had launched a full assault on me during the last two years, and I wasn't going back. I was afraid of what he might do to the kids, violence-wise.

I took the victim's shroud off my shoulders. I had work to do on myself internally and with my children. I was going to try not to whine about him anymore. Nor was I going to dwell on the pain he had caused me except to share it in court. But before I could contact a lawyer, he had his brother serve me divorce papers. His brother said Ken would tear up the papers if I agreed to stay married. Ken had the kids when Joe arrived. I had a black eye from catching a softball with my face, and an empty bottle of wine lay on the floor.

I had to protect the kids.

My fairy tale shattered. I had nothing left to lose except my children, and by God, I was not going to lose them!

I called a lawyer.

Ken played the right card when he went to Chrysalis, a women's advocacy center, to find an awesome female lawyer for the divorce. But she quickly withdrew her counsel, and Ken went pro se. I was not confident that if I were in a same-sex relationship with a woman, the court would see me as fit to parent. Jerry Falwell and the religious fundamentalists had TV shows and were getting into politics. "We are in a moral freefall," they said. Out lesbians were not getting their children in court. After three lawyers and thousands of dollars, the divorce was finalized. I kept Melo updated on the divorce process and even tried to get a French position on the East Coast before I learned I couldn't leave the state with the children without Ken's consent.

Chapter 21

Between visits to the court for the dissolution and custody, I had time away from it all when Ken had the kids, and I went to stay with Mom. We quickly got on the same page and renewed our relationship. Her mothering and concern for my welfare felt warm. However, I did leave out that I was in communication with Melo.

After Mom's divorce, she was also getting her priorities together without a man for the first time in her life. When I learned she had taken classes at the U of M, I was proud of her and felt like I could conquer the world too. She told me about her social studies class of three hundred students and how she got As. Mom could have done anything, given the chance. She took the bus to her job with the city of St. Paul, bought a house, and began divorce proceedings along with Al-Anon meetings.

She invited me to a "Take Back the Night March" downtown. It was crowded—our shoulders bumped each other's. There was a buzz of feminine voices around me as one group yelled, "Break the silence!" and our group answered, "Stop the violence!"

Mom held her sign that said, "Stand together against sexual assault and domestic violence!" She had an intense focus on carrying a banner for women's rights. Her short brown hair bounced in the marching breeze.

I felt encouraged when I looked over at her. Beautiful and determined, she hurried me along when I lagged.

My sign read, "Society teaches 'don't get raped' rather than 'don't rape'!" Mom and I locked arms so we would not lose each other. I mimicked her body language. She led me as never before into the world of strong women.

Difficulties had dominated our past relationship. She did not like Ken and his Jesus talk. The gifts of the Spirit in the charismatic movement were the last straw. She'd thought he and I were proselytizing. He'd proposed on the phone when I was in Winona at college, and he was in Pierre. He even picked out a wedding date so it wouldn't interfere with his summer schedule. When I'd informed Mom on the phone, she'd blown up.

"What?! You're marrying him? He's such a phony! And you have a date? Well, when you want something, you go for it, and you don't care about anyone else's feelings." And she'd hung up. A half hour later, she'd called and solemnly apologized and said we should plan the wedding together.

But walking with her arm in arm under the illumination of the downtown streetlights, warmth radiated throughout my body. I felt a bit vindicated for the pain we'd both struggled with separately and together. We had previously spent hours getting to know each other, drinking wine, and sharing horror stories of our husbands' violence.

A few marchers held candles. People stood along the sidelines, some cheering, some not. Mom held her chin high. It was empowering to be in that marching group with her.

"Mom, look!" I pointed. We protesters stopped in front of a strip club. "That's Scheiks."

We stood and shouted our slogans facing the white Arabian-styled building with balconies and round turrets. The cops moved in. I'm not sure if they were protecting us or the men exiting the club and getting into their limos.

Drums pounded to the rhythm of our chants.

Another sign said, "Fewer than 50 percent of these crimes are reported to the police. It's time to make a change."

It was exhilarating to walk through downtown Minneapolis with my mom, who was wearing a satisfied smile. And I felt liberated walking past men who were yelling, "Go home and cook dinner!" We kept walking, unaffected by their jeering.

These groups were just one more piece of evidence that I was not alone in this world. Each step brought me closer to the fact that I could find happiness.

Chapter 22

The day for the closing on the sale of the house arrived. I was prepared and stronger, no longer willing to be the victim. This house was never a home; it was a boxing ring. Moving on for me was getting rid of it. I did my research and hired a no-nonsense lawyer to close the deal for me because anything involving Ken and money would be a battle.

Boxes were packed and stacked in the living room. After writing letters back and forth, Ken took the table, the ladderback chairs, and the king-sized bed. I put a deposit down on a three-bedroom on Nicollet Avenue, my first rental home.

Sliding the closet door aside, I pulled out a dark red dress with a V-neck and a gathered empire waist. The house was quiet. The kids were at school and Paul at the day care. Searching down deep in my large underwear drawer, I dug around for a good pair of nylons. That drawer had housed souvenirs and trinkets from the beginning of our marriage. The turquoise squash-blossom necklace Ken had bought me lay tarnished in a light-pink quilted jewelry divider along with a gold wedding ring. My hand spread out like a fan inside one leg of the pantyhose as I scanned for runs in the sunlight. With steam rollers in my hair, I felt butterflies in my stomach.

The lawyer was expensive, $500 per hour. I planned to pay for his services and my rent with half of the money from the sale. I told him what I wanted, which was to be fair and split things right down the middle after all fees were paid.

Ken picked the realtor, a ministry friend of both of ours. She'd visited us in our Pierre home several times. Her husband was Ken's former boss, so things were stacked against me. Plus, the buyers were ministry folks whom I admired. Ken knew that. He was up to his usual cunning, setting the stage in his favor. My confidence had grown in the preceding months. Finally, I made decisions for myself and my kids.

I chose my battles and eliminated one by allowing Ken to take all the money his mother had given us when we bought our first house, even though legally, half was mine. With my divorce decree in hand, my focus was on getting my small half of the house's sale.

Unfortunately for him, I was not the unresponsive milquetoast anymore. I knew that victimization had structured many of my relationships, and I told my lawyer not to give in under any circumstances on certain issues. History told me Ken was nervous about me getting any money. To him, money was power, and if I had any, he could not control me. Even though we were no longer married, he continued his attempts to dominate and control the kids.

What he did not know, and nobody else did, is that when I lost everything, I started to get my power back. I had nothing else to lose. All my former hopes and dreams—living in a colonial home by the ocean, teaching and taking classes on the East Coast, raising a happy family, maintaining close spiritual friendships, buying fresh live lobster in a bin at the dock—that idyllic East Coast life was gone. I had lost everything that had once mattered most to me, and now I was going to the closing of our last home together. I was battered and sad, but I had some ammunition and was ready for combat. My reputation among our mutual Christian friends was mostly shattered. I had nothing to lose and nobody to impress.

The deep-oak conference table seemed forty feet long on the second floor of the real estate agency. At the far end of the table sat my friends-turned-adversaries. Our mutual friend, who played the guitar and told great jokes, was sitting there respectfully. His demeanor had often made me laugh, like most of those charismatic leaders'. And his classy wife had inspired me to think about starting a master's in education. She had done it, and that was enough to inspire me to go for mine. They were quietly sitting there, and as I walked in, they gave me a warm smile, but absent was the hug I normally got from them. I had no idea what had been said to them before the meeting.

Swiping a hand through my bouncy curls, I sat down in my conservative red dress with black shoes and nylons. Ken stood in the middle of the room like a conductor ready to entertain, smiling at me and everyone else in the room, as if he already had the upper hand. I breathed short breaths. The flicker of the fluorescent lights irritated me. My very well-prepared lawyer shuffled papers. Before the closing, I'd told him exactly what I wanted and that he should do most of the talking.

Still standing, Ken started. "Mary Beth, I see that your lawyer is here. I don't need one." He gestured to the far end of the table with a smile, "Just my friends in Christ, whom I've known for years." The realtor stood and started the proceedings. She asked Ken to take a seat.

My lawyer began. "Here we are making a simple transaction right down the middle." His hand drew a line in front of him. His bigness was camouflaged behind a blue suit and slicked-back dark hair. "So, let's get started."

After Ken made ridiculous requests and played up to our friends like it was for them that he was there, my lawyer stood up. He raised his voice and started walking alongside the long table with papers raised in his hands, gesturing up and down. "So here we are. Do we have a deal, or do we walk out of here without a deal?"

When Ken and the realtor started to protest, my lawyer threatened to end the meeting. Ken, the realtor, and the couple just sat and stared at him and me. The smiles disappeared.

After the unpaid mortgage, liens, and foreclosure were deducted, I walked out with only a few thousand dollars. That is what I received to start a new life, after being a joint owner of four beautiful homes in our thirteen years of marriage.

Chapter 23

Things came together after the sale of the house. That house crumbled, and now my house was made of steel, a product of World War II. The house had no basement, and everything—even the cupboards—were made of steel. I was not going to let anyone take my house away again. It had been two years since we had moved to Minneapolis and three years since I had met Melo. Minneapolis Public Schools offered me an eight-tenths position teaching French at Washburn and South high schools. I celebrated with piano lessons for my kids and less welfare and food stamps for that year. Plus, Melo and I talked about her moving to Minneapolis.

Up until ten o'clock at night with my books on my lap, I tried to prepare four different classes: two beginner French classes, a level two, and a level three. In-school preparation time was eaten up traveling from one school to the next, but the salary was great; I was thankful and did not complain. Teaching was exhilarating and challenging and gave me a sense of power. I oversaw teaching French to four classrooms of students. With that responsibility, I had a sense of control and authority.

Gabrielle had her room, and the boys shared a room. The big master bedroom with the Priscilla curtains in the first house I could call my very own lifted my spirits. I felt proud of the first home that I had rented myself.

As a new resident of Minnesota, I needed to take classes at the University of Minnesota to update my teaching license. I enrolled right away and began a five-year degree for a master's in second languages and cultures. Evening classes took me away from my kids. Somehow, I arranged for someone to babysit, even if it was Gabrielle's friend who was only one year older. Gabrielle was eleven, Chris was eight, and Paul was five years old.

There were other expenses, like a mouthpiece to protect my teeth from grinding; that was $900. It was hard to teach French with the splint in my mouth. My fingernails grew long because I was not biting them. I had my hair cut and permed to chin length.

I was eager to see Melo, to hear her voice speak forcefully and see her gaze penetrate deep inside me. It had been a few months since I saw her in New England while interviewing for jobs. We just could not be apart. The passion I felt for Melo was far beyond anything I'd felt for Ken. We called two times a week at the most and wrote letters more often. We even sent audio cassette tapes of each other singing and walking through the park having a one-sided conversation.

She showed her love for me and the kids by quitting her job in Massachusetts and preparing to drive to Minnesota.

In a tizzy, I danced around the steel house and put an extra single mattress and box spring on the floor in my room for appearances. She called me along the way as she crammed the 1,200 miles into two days.

I could not wait to sleep next to her and have her hold me. She pulled up in her new aerodynamic blue 1986 Mustang packed with her belongings, including a windsurfing board tied to the top. She wore a tired smile on her face.

"Oh, Melo!" I squealed. "I can't believe you're here!" My pink nightgown flowed as I ran down the long steps. We embraced on Nicollet Avenue, went inside, and held each other all night. I felt like I was in heaven. She blazed back into my life, and we began a sexual relationship. I told my friends, family, and children that we were just friends. No one asked if we were anything else.

In the morning before the kids rose, I sat up in bed and said, "Melo, what a long trip. Sorry we couldn't go back to Rhode Island. I tried." I cleared my throat. "I probably sent over fifty cover letters with my resume, you know."

I watched her look through the suitcase for something to wear. "I know, Mare. You told me on the phone how you'd go to the library on Sundays and get the *Boston Globe* and look for job openings," she said in a singsong half-teasing voice, her head tipping from side to side.

"I just want you to know I tried. I did! It is my first time applying for a job."

"I know." She started pulling on her jeans and t-shirt.

"I would have preferred Barrington or anyplace on the East Coast. I'm still sick about losing that colonial home."

She ran her fingers through her hair in front of the mirror.

"Are you listening? Melo?" I knew she was anxious.

With a big grin, she put her hand to her ear. "I hear some movement out there!"

I jumped out of bed and ran to the locked bedroom door. She got there first.

"Melo's here!" I blared, hoping they would be excited.

Melo walked casually out the door in her bare feet, and I followed her in my robe. Chris ran to look, stopped, and opened his arms in a big jump into her arms. Gabrielle politely greeted her. Little five-year-old Paul said, "Dad's not going to like this," but crisscrossed over for a hug. Melo got down on one knee in front of him.

"We're going to have so much fun!" Her eyes darted to each child.

"Like what?" asked Paul.

She put her hand on his curly light-brown hair. "Well, how about you and I go fishing?"

Chapter 24

"Here, put on this Michael Jackson tape!" Melo suggested with giant eyes. Standing in the gray-carpeted living room, she held up the self-made cassette tape of her favorites. The afternoon sun from the south picture window outlined her profile. Her curly perm framed her head. Smiling to myself, I noticed that her nose still reminded me of Sean Penn.

Chris and Paul bounded right in, hopping to the music, "Man in the Mirror." Melo made comical facial expressions, and her practiced moves jerked and paused right in time to the music. Chris tried to imitate Melo's smooth Michael Jackson moonwalk. Gabrielle needed coaxing off the couch where she sat with Cinnamon, her white-and-tan spotted cat. Melo's sheltie, Ayla, barked in excitement. Melo had appeared one day with her newly purchased puppy. I was OK with more noise and confusion. There we were, bouncing and jumping to the next song, "Thriller," to see who could make the silliest scary dance move. I twirled Paul in the air by his leg and arm and gently landed him on the carpet, then engaged him in a wrestling match.

I cherished these family times; Melo temporarily lifted my guilt of lying to the kids about my affair with her and my love for her. I put the guilt away in a bottom drawer that I opened now and then. With a dish towel wrapped around my waist, I took out my French cookbook, butter, flour, eggs, and apples, and made *generon*, an easy dessert that everyone liked. The aroma of apple cake filled my California-styled home. Baking was a way for me to get quick praise with a finished product.

"We used to have dessert all the time in Pierre," Gabrielle noted as she leaned on the kitchen door.

"I know, honey, but I'm teaching now and going to classes in the evening. It's too tiring to make a dessert every day." Ken had wanted a dessert every evening in Pierre. Cooking was my main source of praise from Ken, so I did a lot of it as I sought to be the happy homemaker. He loved my quiche lorraine and bragged about it to his friends and relatives. I entertained his clients with French onion soup and creamed veal. That was all I knew. My mom had complete meals, down to the hand-squeezed orange juice, lined up on the counter every morning for us six kids. In the fifties and sixties, moms did not work in small-town Pierre, especially Catholic moms.

Melo, the kids, and I all sat down at my grandmother's hand-me-down dining table. Eating dessert in the middle of the day was one of the many rules that I enjoyed breaking.

"Stop smacking!" Paul yelled.

"Smack! Smack!" Chris mimicked the noise with a giggle.

"Stop!" Paul started crying. "Stop it you—you apple face!"

Gabrielle smiled behind her hand. "This apple cake is yummy, Mom. Better than apple pie!"

"Thank you, honey."

"Mom!" Paul whined again.

"Paul, why don't you go eat in the living room," Melo said.

"You aren't my mom!"

"Yes, I am, when your mom is busy," Melo said in a sudden parental role, as she took on an avuncular air with Paul. She picked up Paul's plate and walked into the living room, which was still part of the dining room, an L-shaped area.

"Paul!" I scolded from around the kitchen corner. "You listen to what Melo says to you."

"I'm telling Dad."

"Go ahead," I said in a monotone voice, then turned back into the kitchen to hide my frustration and tears. Even when Ken was not here, he was present in my home.

Ken started calling several times a day. Every time the phone rang, I jumped.

"Hello, Mary Beth. How are you on this fine day?"

"Fine." I hated his fake salesperson voice.

"Can I talk to Chris?"

I paused and held the receiver away from my face. Chris was outside on his skateboard. It annoyed me that Ken called whenever he felt like it. "He's not available," I said before looking outside for Chris. Gabrielle glanced up at me, brushed her bangs away from her face, and went back to reading her book on the couch.

"Really! Are you sure?"

Now I could feel the heat rising in my body. His controlling questioning was loathsome. All I squeaked out was, "Yes."

"Well, then I'll call back in an hour," he shouted.

"No, I'll—" *Click* went his line. These multiple calls per day had been going on for months.

After dinner and homework, we got the kids ready for bed. Melo put Chris down. I heard them telling jokes and laughing.

As usual, I lay next to Paul in the boys' bedroom.

"Should we say prayers, honey?"

"Dear Jesus, thank you for Mom, Dad, and Grandma. Help me have a good sleep tonight. Amen."

"How was your day, sweetheart?" I asked in the dark, hoping he would talk about his crying.

He turned toward me. "Mom? I don't like Melo telling me what to do."

"She's only helping Mommy, and she loves you, sweetheart."

"Well, I don't love her."

I paused. "And I do. Night, night." I rose from his single bed and pulled the covers up to his chin. "Oh, and I'm talking to Chris and Gabrielle about teasing you."

"Night, Mom."

Shutting the sliding steel door gently, I thought, *Of course, he does not love her. She is taking his daddy's place, in one sense.* The problem was one I took seriously—I needed to start seeing things through the kids' eyes more.

I shuffled across the hallway's gray carpet to Gabrielle's door. "Hey, sweetheart."

She glanced up at me from her book. "The dessert was good, Mom." She patted her tummy.

I sat down on the bed next to her cat and stroked him. He purred and lifted his back to my scratching. "How was your day?"

"It was OK. I miss Daddy." Her voice shook, and she continued to look at her book.

"I know. This is hard." She still did not look at me. I wasn't sure how much to tell her, so I changed the subject. "Gabrielle. Can you lay off teasing Paul? He's only five." She nodded. I kissed her forehead and slipped out.

Melo and I snuggled into my newly purchased waterbed; we intertwined our legs. She took my splint off the end table, put it into her mouth, and started talking nonsense with my plastic mouthpiece flapping up and down.

"Stop it, Melo," I laughingly whispered. "Give that back." I fake punched her shoulder. We discussed the day in each other's arms.

"I'm sorry that Paul was a stinker with you, Melo."

"I understand what he's thinking. I would be mad at me too." She laughed. "Well, not too mad. I'm so funny!" I muffled a giggle so the kids wouldn't think we were having too much fun.

We discussed Paul's sensitive hearing. I felt that the yelling I'd done with Ken since he was born had affected him.

In the back of my mind, I thought about the classwork I needed to prepare for tomorrow, but I was more concerned about Paul.

"The screaming must have affected him."

"I'm sure it did, Melo." I reached over and put my hand through her curls and pushed the sad feeling away. "Thanks, Melo, for being with me and the kids, for being fun. I love you." I began to have hope for my future as I held her head in my hands and kissed her on both cheeks and then on the lips. Her neck turned red.

"Now it's time to go into your bed."

Chapter 25

When the kids left for Ken's place every other weekend, Melo and I danced at Ladies' Night and Rumours, both gay bars in St. Paul that were far away from anyone I knew. I anticipated the richness of my lesbian life without naming it. My excitement of pulling into the Ladies' Night parking lot mounted as we approached the dimly lit entrance.

"Are you still feeling some resentment, Melo, about coming here to Minneapolis?" I asked as she parked the Mustang.

"I'm OK, Mare, but—"

"You know, Melo"—I turned toward her—"I wish we didn't have to keep our love a secret."

"Yeah?"

"I mean, here at Ladies' Night, I feel free to love you in the open, kiss you in the open." She reached over and kissed me hard and long.

"Mare? As long as the yellow star shines, I just want you and me to be together. I want to shout it out to everyone. I don't like keeping it under wraps."

"But Melo, you know how scary Ken is."

She took a deep breath and opened the car door. "Let's go!"

It was fun being carded; the anticipation of dancing with Melo and even dancing alone made me tingle. I relished breaking rules on the dance floor. At the bar, I got my usual rum and Coke; we made our way to a table and sat down with our drinks.

"Everybody Dance Now" was playing. I got up at once and moved every joint in my body. Melo watched and joined with her take-over-the-whole-floor style. We deliberated which songs to request and came up with Prince's "Kiss" and Paula Abdul's "Opposites Attract."

Right away, Melo stood up and started looking around for her new work friends from Little Caesars. Her dark balloon pants stood out and flowed as she walked. I loved how she ignored what people thought. When Michael Jackson's music started, she commanded the dance floor for a few seconds from one side to another, then stopped and gestured for me to come and join her. Melo was at her best when she had an audience. Our legs wove in and out like an accordion. She clowned around when her friends arrived. We danced for the next few hours. As always when dancing, I was transported from the present to a cloud of music where my body, not my mind, controlled my movements. I began unfolding my wings and trying new expressions of myself. My hand motioned for her to come near me. She leaned down, so I could talk over the music. Instead, I imprinted myself on Melo as she imprinted on me. We flowed in close proximity around each other's movements. I took her chin and gave her a long kiss, showing everyone in the club that she was mine. I was thrilled to be with her and felt very at home in St. Paul's gay bars.

Melo kept in touch with her work friends from Little Caesars and St. Joseph's Home for Children. I kept up my jogging with Debra and classes at the U. We jogged along Minnehaha Creek, sharing stories about our families. Her short blond hair bobbed with the rhythm of our steps hitting the pavement. She lifted my spirits with positive feedback on my school troubles. Debra worked on her master's in education too. Her acceptance of my relationship with Melo helped me make baby steps toward my true self.

My teaching job was stressful. Certain students and parents took advantage of my inexperience. One of my best French students started skipping class. When I saw her in the hallway, I said in French, "Tu me manques!"

She said, "What does that mean?"

I said back, "I miss you!" When her parents came in after school, I made the rookie mistake of telling them first thing that she was failing. She had been one of my top students. The parents became irate and began ordering me around my office. From that day on, I always started a parent or student meeting with a positive.

Despite the chaos at school, with Melo's help, I managed the bedlam at home.

Chapter 26

"Mare, how are we doing Christmas? Do I bring a gift to your mom's?" Melo questioned me on Christmas Eve morning. She also wanted to know who would be there and what she should bring as a gift. I wanted my family to accept her and for her to feel comfortable.

We all hung around the kitchen and dining room; the tree was lit, and a Perry Como record played on the turntable.

"Lucy is the one who likes me, right?"

"Yes, Melo, she likes you a lot." I gave Melo a long look with a finger pointing from my heart to hers to let her know I also loved her.

"She likes me too; she brought crab legs from the Boston Sea Party to my sleepover," Chris said as he noticed my hand signals and smiley side glance.

"Hey, you!" I grabbed Chris and tackled him to the carpet.

"Mom, are we going to watch movies and eat popcorn with Grandma like we did last week?"

I rose from the carpet and pulled Chris up. "Not this time, honey, just eat delicious hors d'oeuvres and open a bunch of presents for you!" I said as I pulled the pâté out of the fridge and took the brick weight off it. The brick helped the pâté firm up so I could slice it nicely.

"Yeah!" Paul yelled at the same time, clapping his hands and jumping in a circle. "I love presents and parties. Hope I get a *Star Wars* spaceship."

"Me too." Melo started clapping with Paul.

"Melo, do you want to roll out sugar cookies with Chris and Paul? The dough is in the fridge."

"I want to, Mom!" Gabrielle said as she came in from the living room.

With a smirk, Melo said, "Only if we can all eat the cookie dough. Oh, and should we bring some cookies to dinner at your mom's?"

"Yes." I opened a kitchen drawer and dug way back. "Here's a Santa cookie cutter." I held it up. "He's holding a bag of toys."

"No, I don't think so," Melo added as she surveyed the cookie cutter. "*She's* holding a bag of clothes for Melo." Melo gave a fake laugh, as though she'd tricked us.

Gabrielle rolled her eyes.

We joined in with Perry Como for the first line of "White Christmas," singing in exaggerated operatic voices.

"When are we going to Grandma's?"

"Not until two o'clock. I have to make sure my French country pâté is ready."

We loaded the car with pâté, cookies, wine, and gifts.

On the drive to Mom's, the kids sat quietly in the back seat of Melo's car while we listened to KDWB on the radio. I glanced sideways at Melo. I was filled with love and tenderly took her hand while watching the gentle snowfall. The kids started whispering in the back seat. Chris and Gabrielle were gesturing at us and snickering. I turned around, red faced, and snapped:

"What? Two women can hold hands!"

They were silenced by my angry retort and did not respond. I felt a deep chasm between me and my kids at that moment. They saw something. Yet, I wanted them to believe that we were just friends. I did not want Ken to be right and me to be the liar. The music played while no one talked.

I looked away from Melo, out the car window, my fist under my chin. They were not buying the "just friends" line we had been giving them. I felt ashamed and wondered how to keep up the charade when inside I was bursting with passion for Melo. I was fearful.

All Mom knew and chose to believe was that we were friends. I know she was grateful that Ken was no longer in her life either. My mom and siblings, Lucy and Frank, loved me even with my fragmented information about my relationship with Melo.

"Hey, MB, how ya doing?" Lucy came up to me and gave me a big hug. Then she whispered in my ear, "So glad you got rid of that asshole husband of yours." She at once turned to Melo and hugged her. "Melo, I think it's wonderful that you are here in Minneapolis with Mary Beth! Welcome to your first Spray family Christmas!"

Melo relaxed. Mom came over with her apron on and hugged me. "Hope you're all hungry! Hi, Melo." Melo handed her the wine.

"Oh, thank you, Melo!" Mom put her hand on Melo's back to usher her into the house. "Where are my grandchildren?"

"Here we are, Grandma!" Paul shouted.

Frank showed them all the wrapped presents. "Merry Christmas, MB, Melo. How's teaching?" he asked.

"We're all doing well," I said, trying to include Melo in the conversation.

"Here's the latest." He handed me a VHS tape labeled *Chris and Paul's Hockey*.

"You are awesome to do this for me, Frank. Thanks."

As my family gave out presents, Melo took the gift handed to her while sitting in the blue-flowered wingback chair.

She was dressed in nice slacks and a cuffed shirt. She waited with excited eyes and held her breath for the signal to open her big wrapped gift. My family and kids watched. Beneath the wrapping paper came a tapestry cloth purse with a hard leather handle and a snap-clip closure. Heat rose to my face.

"Thank you, Helen," she said with a dry fake smile.

Mom didn't notice and continued handing out presents. She wasn't familiar with Melo enough to see that this purse was far from Melo's style or personality and that Melo didn't care for feminine things. She would have liked anything but a purse. I knew Melo deeply, but of course Mom did not get Melo's butch vibe from us. We presented Melo to my family as a housemate. I wanted Mom to know Melo as I did: the crazy, fun-loving, sporty gal.

"She doesn't know that we're lovers, Mare," Melo said to me later in bed. Melo always tried to look on the bright side.

I started laughing. "That purse is hilarious, Melo. I would never be caught dead with it!"

"It looks like an old-lady purse." Melo stood up and pranced around the room with the hard leather handle over her shoulder, the snap clasp in her armpit.

"How does it look?" She jumped on her single bed doing spread-eagle leg poses, holding the purse with each jump.

"Come here beside me in bed, you silly goose." I embraced her under the covers and pulled out a small box.

"For me?" She tore open the small package, which revealed tiny diamond-pierced earrings. She handed me a wooden jewelry box with Renaissance dancers painted on the top and a pair of tasseled woven slippers that came halfway up my calves.

The presents seemed to assuage our denial in the car today.

"I love you, Mare."

"I love you. Melo, how are we going to do this relationship of ours?"

"Maybe we could move back to Rhode Island? I want to get away from in-your-face Ken." She lay back on the bed with one leg crossed over her knee.

"I tried, Melo; the court won't let me leave the state." I would have loved to still be living in Rhode Island. The sound and smell of the ocean were gone. But I had support in Minnesota through my family and friends like Debra. Maybe I was settling for Minneapolis.

"I thought things would be better after the divorce and living together. I can't get away from him. He makes me so mad." She slammed her fist into the bed.

Her visceral expression of anger startled me.

Chapter 27

Melo helped with the finances each month. I did not ask for anything, and it was a pleasant shock for me to have the extra $200, since Ken was not paying child support consistently and our visits to court produced nothing. Ken just lamented that he wasn't making anything, and somehow the court seemed slow and had little backbone.

Melo's new job at St. Joe's matched her degree, which was youth ministry; we joined a St. Joe's softball team. Melo was athletic, and I was embarrassingly lousy even though I used to play the sport. I was inhaling the women's community in Minneapolis. We went to parties. I joined a lesbian writers' group and made friends of my own.

After Ken's phone calls, sometimes Gabrielle started chewing the inside of her cheek as Ken did. When he called, the kids all ran to the phone excited to talk to him. They were still working out this family separation. But sometimes my oldest had a blank expression that I could not read. She stared straight ahead and said nothing. What was he saying to her?

"Are you OK, honey?" She looked away without answering.

Chris constantly teased Paul. I tried to keep track of their reactions but failed miserably.

Melo and I went to RadioShack and bought an attachment to my tape player to plug into the landline phone in my bedroom so we could listen in on Ken's phone calls with the kids. I was worried he might try to manipulate or hurt them with his talk. He called whenever he wanted, and purposely rang during dinner or when he knew we had a planned activity.

Ring-ring. "I'll get it!" Chris yelled. Melo excused herself from the table to press start on the tape recorder in our bedroom.

"Hi, Chubbs!"

"Hi, Daddy!" Chris smiled as he talked. "We're eating taco pie." His eyes lit up.

"Sounds yummy. What did you do today?"

"Went skateboarding with Melo."

"Are you careful?"

"Yeah." He jumped from side to side, imitating Melo.

"Can I talk to Paul?"

Paul skipped to the phone. "Melo took me fishing again!" he almost screamed.

"Fun!"

"And I caught another crayfish!" He held out his hands.

Gabrielle came to the phone. Her cheeks were red. She spoke in a soft tone. "Hi, Dad."

"Is everything OK over there, honey? I worry about you."

"Yeah? Why?" Her back was to us; her finger wrapped ringlets with her hair.

"I'm just concerned . . . now that Melo's there in the house."

The tape turning in the bedroom eased my anger a bit. "Mare, let's keep track of the number of calls every day until your child support court date in two weeks," said Melo. "Here's some graph paper. Between the two of us, we'll get a picture of his intrusions for the judge." She pulled out the paper and wrote the days of the week on one side.

"See, it's easy."

"Well, I don't want the kids to find out."

Melo walked over to me and embraced me. "We'll take care of this guy's obnoxious phone-calling."

We started keeping track of every phone call and the time of day. In a couple of weeks, we had the evidence of his intrusive behavior to present to the judge.

"First of all, sir, do you have anything to say to start?" the judge asked.

Ken stood up. Since his former lawyer withdrew, he had been coming to court pro se to declare how little finances he had to pay child support. "Yes, Your Honor." His face became serious. He looked down and declared,

"Melo came to live with my wife . . . err . . . ex-wife, Mary Beth. I'm support-ing the kids financially the best I can."

There was no response from the judge.

With my lawyer sitting next to me, I stood up and started reading, my paper trembling.

"Sunday, March 15, 10:05 a.m., Ken called right before church, then again at 4:25 p.m. and again at 7:30 p.m., the third time that day. Monday, March 16, he called at 7:30 a.m. before school and again at 5:30 during dinner."

Ken stood up and walked toward me. "No, that's not true, Your Honor!" His finger was in the air.

"Sit down! Let her finish!"

"On Tuesday, March 17, he called again, at 7:00 a.m. this time. Then after school at 4:30 p.m. and late at 9:30 p.m. The kids were all in bed. He even called on the morning of last New Year's Day when he had the kids!"

Ken tried to interrupt me several more times during my reading. I kept reading, but before I finished, the judge stopped me.

"That's enough, I have the picture." She looked stern and businesslike.

"Your Honor, I have to reiterate that this so-called list of Mary Beth's is not true." He looked around the courtroom again and slammed his hand on the table before him. "It is categorically not true!"

"I have made my decision." She tapped the bottom of her papers two times on her judge's bench.

"Mr. Wilson, from now on, you will call no more than once per day. And only after 6:30 p.m."

The very next day, the phone rang. "I'll get it!" Gabrielle yelled as she got up to answer the phone on the piano.

"Wait!" I said. "It's six o'clock. I'll get it." I picked up the receiver with clammy hands. "Hello?"

"Can I speak to Gabrielle, please?" his fake low voice demanded.

My mouth was dry. "No, not until six thirty." I cleared my throat and kicked the steel wall with the toe of my sneakers.

"Come on. I have a meeting tonight. You're going to keep me from talking to my children?"

"You know what the judge said," I fired at him and hung up, my heart beating a hundred times a minute. I leaned against the wall and my tight jaw unlocked. No one heard me.

At six twenty-five, *ring!*

My jaw tightened again as I nodded to Melo. She picked it up. "Hello?" She listened for a half minute. "Call back in five minutes."

He called again. Gabrielle talked only for a few minutes.

"That was short."

"Yeah, he said he could only talk for a minute because he had a meeting, and you wouldn't let him talk earlier."

"Hmmm." I felt more in control of my household.

It was one of many times I wanted to explain to her what the judge had said and how Ken was violating my space, but I kept silent. I did not want the kids to be in the middle. He would just deny it, and they would be left with questions pitting one parent against the other.

Chapter 28

The softball skipped right toward me. Trying to concentrate, I bent my knees and focused, my open mitt in front of my chest. Coming, coming–bounce!

I fumbled.

The woman on first base threw her cap on the dirt.

The second-base player to my left groaned, "Ah, come on! That was an easy catch!" The team exited the field having lost the game because I messed up. Melo ran over to me.

"That's OK, Mare." She put her arm over my shoulders, her gloved hand hanging down over me and her other hand in her jeans pocket. I was mortified. I did not look at anyone; I just wanted to go home. I vowed to myself to never come back.

"But your friends are going to hate me." I adjusted my ponytail as well as my new jeans. It was 1987, a year after Melo drove from Massachusetts to live with me.

She stopped midgait and turned to me, her eyes softening as she looked deep into mine.

"No, Mare, no one hates you."

Two players were already giggling. Angela put her mitt on top of Roberta's head and said, "I glove you." Angela grinned at Roberta. Angela's soft, long brown ponytail swished as she played with her glove. Others smiled as they watched.

"Angela's pretty," I whispered to Melo.

"She is?" Melo's eyes opened wide and turned around to look at her again.

I stood awkwardly among them, not making eye contact while Melo went over to Michelle.

"I glove you!" Roberta declared to Angela in front of me. Roberta's wavy black hair touched her shoulders. She took a pack of Virginia Slims from her back pocket, shook out a single cigarette, put it to her puffy lips, and squinted one eye as she lit. Angela bragged about the beer roll of fat around her waist as she lifted her shirt for everyone to see.

They walked to Roberta's light-blue 280Z. A two-seater.

As I watched them leave, I noticed Melo and Michelle laughing. Michelle had her back to me. Her head was cocked toward Melo. As I approached, Michelle took off her cap.

"So, you and Mary Beth aren't a couple?" She combed her fingers through her short dark hair and the rat tail that fell down her back. Then she fitted her cap back on. She wore black-rimmed glasses and had five small earrings up the outside of her ear: a silver star, a turquoise stone the size of a nail head, a fleur-de-lis, a peace sign, and a piece of Black Hills gold.

"No, we're just friends," Melo said.

"Well"—Michelle stared intently—"you both sure act like a couple."

My insides twisted with fear. I thought it was becoming increasingly obvious, even to people we barely knew. I had to figure out who to come out to, and who to keep in the dark. It was becoming complicated. I wanted to be free and honest about my love for Melo. But my fear took over. I cleared my throat. Melo shrugged and changed the subject. These were her friends. I wanted secrecy about our relationship, and Melo was moving toward coming out. That was what I had hoped for, but on the other hand, I was not so sure.

Michelle, an out lesbian, had been talking to Melo about LGBTQ+ issues. I noticed they were talking quietly. Melo spun around. "We're going to the movies. Want to join us?"

"Yeah, of course. What movie?" I asked as I moved one step closer to Melo.

"How about *Fatal Attraction*? Have you seen it?"

"No. And I have never gone to a movie in the afternoon except with the kids to cool off in the air-conditioning. Sounds like fun." I was intrigued to break one of my innocuous rules. Michelle stepped in front of me. I noticed her Doc Martens, her jeans rolled up and tucked above them.

"I'm on my motorbike. Do you want to hop on the back, Melo?"

"Thanks, but I'll drive Mary Beth. We'll meet you there?"

In the Mustang, I double-checked to see if it was OK to tag along. Melo said she was not interested in Michelle like that. We talked about the others, and she told me Roberta had left her husband for Angela, and they both had good jobs.

Melo sat between us at the movies. I set my popcorn on the seat next to me, which I rarely do. Usually, I shovel popcorn into my mouth.

I reached over in the dark theater and took Melo's hand. Out of the corner of my eye, I noticed Michelle looking down at our hands. She said nothing. Our fingers were intertwined during the whole frightful movie. I felt brave; my first shy coming-out happened in the dark. I held her hand all the way out into the light. I did not want to lose Melo to this young woman, Michelle. I had to step up my game.

In the car ride back from the Boulevard Theater, Melo stared straight ahead. We started arguing about me coming out and how hard it was for her to pretend and lie.

"Well, what about how I feel? I am right here in your life and your bed except when I'm sent to my little single bed where all I have is my teddy bear, Benjamin." She shook her head silently, and tears streamed down her cheek. "When are you going to stand up for me?"

We pulled up the long driveway and stopped. I leaned over to her and embraced her. "I don't know how this is going to turn out. Melo, what if you want to date a guy? I don't want to be selfish . . ."

"A guy?!" She turned to me and raised her voice. "A guy?"

"I just meant . . ." I bit my thumbnail. "I don't want you to be tied down to me because I don't know who I am . . . I'm just a mom, and maybe a teacher if I get another position." I looked out the window at the steel house to hide my tears. I quickly wiped them with my sweatshirt sleeve. "It will work out, right? It just will." Whenever I felt fear, I would look for Melo's positivity about us. She always assured me even when I doubted where we were headed as a couple.

She perked up. "Yes, it will work out. I know it will. But Mare, you must figure this out. You called that guy for a date during New Year's Eve! Remember?"

"And then you told another man that I wanted a New Year's kiss!" I tried to let her know that she'd encouraged me, as though she knew I was bisexual without me having to declare it.

"Well, did you?"

"Melo, I'm not at all sure what I want."

I took the elastic out of my ponytail, brushed a hand through my perm, and stared at her for a long pause. My eyes filled with tears, I whispered, "You—it's only *you* I want to kiss me, hold me, love me."

Her forehead gently pressed against mine. Her body's natural perfume of soothing outdoor clary sage filled my nostrils. My face was inches from hers.

"I will, Mare."

I wiped my tears on my sleeve again, cleared my throat, and asked, "For how long?"

"Do you see all the stars in the Milky Way at night?" She pointed up to the sky. I smiled because I knew where she was going.

"I will love you, Mary Beth, a hundred times more than the number of stars in the Milky Way."

We walked, arms around each other's waists, into the steel house, straight to my bed, her declaration in my heart. She pulled down my jeans; I kicked them off the bed. We threw our T-shirts across the room. Her soft breasts caressed mine as she hovered above me. She was all giving, as usual, knowing what I liked without talking. She teased me with her breasts, sweeping them up and down my legs, arms, and face. I could smell her sweat. She tasted salty. We held the quiet. I pulled her up so I could look into her eyes. They were piercingly intense. Our breathing quickened as her fingers touched my wetness. She slowly moved down with her tongue, and my insides tightened and quivered to an indescribable climax. Afterward, while I lingered curled up in her arms, she tapped her face and commented, "Now I'm wearing your perfume."

Lovemaking with Melo felt easy. I felt wanted and celebrated.

"Let's go to Figlio's for dinner." Jumping onto the carpet, I did my side kick in the air. It always made Melo laugh. We dressed up, although it took Melo a while to find the right khakis and shirt. I wore a black dress with a big red flower on it and wooden Barbie heels.

After a few minutes' wait, we entered the bright dining room, where I could hear folks in the bar and see the row of tables against the long Lake Street window. The garlic aroma made my stomach growl.

We sat at a white-clothed table and ordered pasta. I'm sure we looked the odd couple on a Saturday night. The energy between us was vibrating. I tossed away my usual worries about what people might think when they encountered us.

"You know, Melo, what we've done so far today feels weird. First, today I am not responsible for kids," I said, counting on my fingers. "We played softball, went to a movie, made love, now we're eating out at my favorite restaurant, and we're going to Ladies' Night to dance!" I declared, holding up my arms in victory.

She giggled. "I know. This is fun, isn't it?"

I leaned forward. "This is the first time in my life that I feel young and free!"

"You better live it up, Mare."

I leaned back in my chair and winked at her as I sipped my cabernet.

"Hey, Mare, I have soccer tomorrow; I joined a women's team."

"Nice. Can I watch sometime?"

"Of course. I love an audience."

The attraction was twofold for me. Every feminine quality about her appealed to me: her breasts and strong body, her soft voice, her long eyelashes, and her childlike innocence. She was not feminine in her dress or mannerisms–or at least she was not what I thought of as feminine. Her clothes were comfortably baggy, T-shirts and cool high-top basketball shoes. She lived her desires even if it meant driving forty minutes to the indoor soccer field. My hero! She did these things for herself, and here I was being the "selfless" mom: taking care of kids, going to school, and working, always needing a babysitter.

"Hey!" She nodded to me. "What are you thinking about?"

"You." My face reddened as I thought of my orgasm that afternoon. I was filled with love and wanted to kiss her but held back. "Should we go?"

We walked in the dark through the parking lot. I almost grabbed her hand when two guys passed us. One said, "Nice tits!"

Without skipping a beat, Melo's eyebrows bunched, and she bellowed, "Nice dick!"

Chapter 29

After a few months, Melo bounced in from work late one evening. Heading straight for the phone, she put her leg over the arm of the chair and leaned back playing with the cord. She was engaged, laughing, and animated. She seemed consumed in an intense conversation. I gave her a quick wave as I looked up from my schoolwork. Our eyes met, but she did not acknowledge me. It was as if she saw right through me. Someone had distracted her. Usually, when she came home, we sat and talked about our days. I didn't even know her schedule anymore.

While correcting papers, I tried to listen, but I could not hear all the sounds she made. I heard happy sounds–the kind she made with me. I couldn't imagine her making sweet sounds to someone else. I pretended to read the French textbook in my lap.

With a big laugh, she jiggled her leg.

The French words in the textbook jumbled before my eyes. I had to prepare for lessons for the following day, and she was enjoying someone else. I told myself to get a grip. I inhaled for six counts and exhaled for another six. I picked up my planner and started writing my feelings:

I am scared. I might be losing Melo. Oh Lord Jesus, help me through this moment. Help me to calm down. I don't want to lose her, like when Ken wrote about Pauline that first year of marriage. I don't want that pain again. What is it about me that makes them look to someone else?

At one point, I glanced over and her neck was red.

I wondered if I was sharing her with someone else. I got up and walked past her into the bathroom. She had a crush on someone. I straightened the hand towel on the rack. Somehow, my thoughts went back to when I'd read Ken's journal that said he loved two women. I sat on the toilet to think. I didn't want to lose her, and I knew I had to fight for her. I had to go back out there and ask her who that was.

When I came out of the bathroom, the phone conversation was over. "Hi, Melo."

She grinned to herself, running the zipper of her jacket up and down. "Hi, Mare."

"Who were you talking to for an hour?" I tried to make my voice soft, but I said it too fast and pushed the word *hour*.

Her face fell. She stared ahead. "That was Angela."

I said nothing. She was younger, and I was a divorced mom. Why wouldn't she have had a crush on someone her age?

"You know, the girl from softball? The one you said was cute."

"Melo!" I stretched out the two syllables of her name and sneered. "Your neck was red!" I tried to suppress the confrontation, as well as my tears.

She narrowed her eyes. "So?"

"Do you have a crush on her?" I tried not to reveal my feelings. I wanted to go to her, but I stayed standing by the couch.

"What do you mean?"

"I know what it means when you have a red neck!" My face tightened. "You used to have a red neck when we talked intimately." I fell back on the couch, hoping she would sit next to me.

"Mare, this is me. I can't help it. I'm just talking to her." She stepped back toward the hall, then turned. "Well, maybe I'm getting a life with my lesbian friends. Maybe I'm coming out to them."

Immediately, I felt abandoned. We went to our separate beds without talking. I lay in the dark. Across our bedroom, I could hear Melo tossing and kicking the covers. I knew she was not asleep yet.

"Melo?"

"Yeah?"

"I love you."

"I love you too, Mare."

"Can I come over?"

"Yeah."

I jumped out of bed in my nightgown and slithered under the warm covers of her single bed. I felt her body under her T-shirt.

Hoping my fears would go away, I hung on to her for dear life.

Chapter 30

"Hey Mare, I'm going out with Angela and Roberta and their friends tonight."

I turned toward her.

"We're going to buy a special screw gun at Home Depot, then steal stop signs and return the screw gun and get our money back." She stood in the doorway of the new home that we had just rented together.

She smiled, and I could tell she was challenging my rules. Stealing signs did not appeal to me. I twirled in a self-conscious Michael Jackson twist. "Melo, I'll miss you. But do I get some time with you this weekend?" I decided that I had to cut out my jealous comments in front of her. I refrained from saying anything about Angela.

"Yeah, we're going dancing at Ladies' Night tomorrow night if you want to join us." She rested her hand on the door frame and threw her jean jacket over her shoulder. I felt a whirl in my groin as I eyed her slim body tucked into baggy, holey jeans and a puffy paisley sweatshirt.

"It's bitter cold out, but yes, I wouldn't miss dancing with you for anything!" My hand pulled her close, and I embraced her with a kiss.

I watched her get into the Mustang. I mulled over how much fun sneaking around in the dark might be. After a cigarette break and a hot cup of Red Zinger on the back steps, I went back to hours of schoolwork and the paper I had to write at the dining room table.

The next night at the bar, she was a hit clowning around. She left me at a table in the center of the smoky room and went to the stage area to entertain us. Her head peeked around a corner sideways; she wore a silly grin, and her permed hair stuck straight up and out on all sides. Her hand appeared from behind the wall above her head. She made it look like someone else's hand as she pulled her own head back behind the wall.

At the first twang of Prince's guitar in "Kiss," we jumped up to take over the dance floor. We spread out at either end and slowly advanced toward each other, twisting and gyrating to the beat. My knees waved in and out with each step while Melo split her legs down to the floor and lifted them in one smooth move. When "Wind Beneath My Wings" came on, we merged. I was happy to be in her arms and out for the evening. In the lesbian bar, where no straights could slap an *L* on my back, I took in the words to Bette Midler's song, Melo's soft cheek next to mine. All my worries disappeared.

She squealed to Michael Jackson's high-pitched shrieks and bounced all around the bar to "The Way You Make Me Feel" in her red-and-black Nike high-tops. I laughed, hoping to not wet my pants. I sat down at our table. I did not see Angela as most of Melo's other friends joined in with her antics.

Sitting on the back step and smoking a cigarette, I contemplated my life so far. Melo was falling through my fingers. I prayed that God would take over my relationship with Melo and work a miracle to bring the fervor back again. I felt alone: me against the hetero and gay world. The terror of losing my children versus losing the love of my life crippled me for a while. I held on to Melo desperately. She dared to do all the things I felt I should not do. I had not met anyone like her. I thought I was getting to be too boring for her. A counselor told me to make a list of my ten top rules and to break one per day.

It was complicated for Melo to be with me and not come out about our sexual relationship. Losing Melo was too much for me to bear, but if I came out, I was confident that Ken would intensify his efforts to keep the kids from me. That was my overwhelming fear, and it was constant. I did not trust him. His family had money and lawyers. Yet, I realized I would need to come out for Melo to still be interested in me. I couldn't strengthen my relationship with her while keeping it hidden.

Internally, I was bursting out. I wanted to tell everyone of my love for her. I could see our relationship changing from Melo, me, and the kids as a family to Melo as a housemate with a separate life and friends. But I remained in the closet, except in my writers' group and queer bars where it was safe. The societal norms on gay rights were slow moving during the late eighties. My lesbian writer-friend took her case to the Minnesota Supreme Court just to keep her child.

But now, being on shaky ground with Melo, all my single parenting and finances slipped back onto my shoulders. As a new Minneapolis Public Schools teacher, I had to start at the bottom, substituting and taking piecemeal part-time teaching positions. All nontenured teachers got a pink slip every May, which upped my anxiety level. I had to file for unemployment and public aid for the summer. I taught summer school and took temporary summer jobs. I wasn't sure that I'd continue to get rent from Melo. Child support was little if any.

I felt like I could do anything with Melo by my side. Without her, I was lost. Or at least I thought I was lost. I had always clung to someone: parents, Ken, Melo. I had never tried life on my own. I was scared to be alone with myself because it meant I would have to love who I was, and I didn't even like myself. All my life, I had looked for the perfect partner.

In 1988, I was not hired back in the fall by MPS. The salary from my new full-time job at the adoption office barely stretched for food. Melo's contribution helped. I was in shock and shame that entire year at not being hired back. I had interviewed at high schools and junior high schools in the metro area and thought I'd been successful. I had notes from students and principals praising my work. To hide my shame, I told friends and family that I wanted to spend more time working on my master's, so I'd taken a year off. But I hadn't taken a year off. I wasn't hired back. Mom helped with the school finances at the U. I was very thankful that she was there for me. I felt her love and support, and it meant the world to me.

In the beginning, Melo had helped with the kids. But by this point, she was rarely around, and I could barely keep up with all their activities: Chris had drum lessons, Gabrielle had her first boyfriend, Paul was forever in front of the TV playing his Nintendo. Melo was increasingly absent, and I missed her. On a whim, I opened the front hall closet to touch her jean jacket. After smelling it, I was warmed by the cigarette odors which hung around its creases. A piece of newspaper poked out of her jacket pocket. Gently, I pulled it out.

Love Lines. Love lines were a pre-cell-phone method of connecting romantically with someone. The interested party would write a one-line declaration using the other person's name. I read the torn piece of newspaper, scanning and searching. My hands shook. Quickly, after glancing at the names, I put it back. There was no A for Angela, nor an M for Mary Beth? I wondered if she'd sent someone a message in the newspaper. But Valentine's was over. I planned on asking her after the kids went to bed that night.

At six in the evening, I walked in the door. Melo and the kids were all home. A savory whiff of a chicken dinner came from the oven. The phone rang in the kitchen. Gabrielle and Chris both raced from the living room.

"I'll get it!" Gabrielle yelled. I heard two sets of legs running. "Give it to me now!"

"May I ask who's calling, please?" Chris asked in a mocking, soft tone, teasing his sister.

Paul's Nintendo plinked on the TV screen; he was engrossed in the *Super Mario Bros.* game. Chris went out the back door while Gabrielle went downstairs to talk on the cordless phone in private. Melo hummed a tune, acknowledged me with a nod, and put her finger where she'd left off on the new recipe she was trying. She did not look back up, so I stayed away. My serotonin deficiency ramped up as I sensed her not wanting to kiss me or talk. That wound felt like a fist grinding.

Upstairs, I put books from my Spanish class on my bed. I took several extension classes in Spanish at the U to enhance my hiring ability. I was glad not to have to prepare dinner that night. I quietly lay down on my bed and closed my eyes. What a busy day I'd had, and I had a long night ahead preparing for the class I was taking after work. I planned on doing my Spanish homework after talking to Melo.

Melo had been trying new recipes. I didn't know what she was thinking anymore. I wondered if she was trying to impress someone. She was gone more, working the weird night shift and being out with her friends. The phone woke me up from my ten-minute reverie.

As I came downstairs, Melo yelled, "Time to eat!"

Melo presented the dinner to us at the dining room table. She brought out a wonderful chicken dish in a cheesy white cream sauce. Heat rose from the Pyrex. What was wonderful about this meal was that Melo had created it. Her familiar giggle warmed my empty stomach.

"I'll have two helpings," Paul said with a parted-teeth smile.

"Paul, let her serve everyone else and then see if there are seconds."

"Are there mushrooms? Cause if there are, I don't want any."

"Chris!" I gave him a warning stare.

Melo stood, serving us with a ladle and fork and adding sauce if we asked for it. She was enjoying our compliments. Then she sat down across from me. Rarely were we all at home like this, sitting and eating together. I sat at the other end of the oval table. I wanted this family time to stay forever, but I had a hard conversation planned for later.

"When do you work tonight, Melo?" Chris asked.

"Not until eleven."

"Don't you get tired and fall asleep in the middle of the night?"

"Sometimes," she said with a smile. "But don't tell my boss."

The phone rang. I glanced at the clock on the kitchen wall. Gabrielle and Chris raced to pick up. Melo and I made eye contact for a second. I felt electricity with her eyes looking at me. She stared a second longer while I took in her energy.

"Hi, Dad. It's Dad!" Chris announced.

"OK, honey," I said.

We finished our meal as each child talked to Ken for a few minutes.

"That was delish, Melo. What cheese did you use?"

"Parmesan. I tried a new recipe." We smiled. Some nights were good in our family. This was perfect. I didn't want much anymore. I didn't need prestige and a fancy colonial. I just wanted harmony at the dinner table, like we had that night.

The kids did the dishes.

After they went to bed, I told her about the love lines that I'd found when invading her jacket. She explained that she had written a poem for Angela but had not sent it to the newspaper.

I wanted her to take me in her arms and talk about all the love poems she'd sent me over the last couple of years, or the secret love poems disguised as prayers when I was still married in Rhode Island. But I got nothing. As I sat on the couch across from her, I bit the skin around my fingernails and knew that something bad was going to happen.

"You just thought about it? Like you're"—I swallowed—"thinking about her a lot."

"Mare, I'm late." She huffed impatiently and swung her legs off the arm of the chair. With her jean jacket crunched in her hand, she walked toward the door. "Oh, and Mare, I'm going to a cabin with friends this weekend."

She turned and left without an explanation or details. I sat there looking at the closed oak door. The next few minutes felt like hours. She usually told the truth. She was really going, and I was not invited. It was my weekend with the kids. She used to always make fun plans for when the kids were away. I wondered why I was intentionally excluded.

The weekend came, and she was gone.

When the kids went to friends' homes, I got in my Toyota hatchback. I did not have the facts right about where Melo had gone. I considered that maybe she was still in town and just staying at Angela and Roberta's apartment.

Many things are pathetic, but few are as bad as me driving up and down the streets of trendy Uptown, crying pitifully and looking for their new apartment and for Melo's car. It was raining and dark, just like my heart. I turned the radio off. The wipers were my music. I prayed. *Lord Jesus, bring her back to me. Keep her attraction to me. Let her realize I need time. Give her patience to stick by me. I just need more time.*

It was pitch black and moonless. My goal was to spot Melo's blue Mustang or one of Roberta's brown or baby-blue sports cars.

Rolling at about ten miles an hour, upset and unglued, I drove on every street from Thirty-First to Thirty-Sixth, and from Hennepin to Lake Calhoun. I let out a piercing scream that shattered the silence. I stopped at what I thought was Roberta and Angela's apartment and stared up at the dark windows on the third floor. Then I drove to the back of the apartment and still saw no familiar sports cars, nor Melo's blue Mustang.

I wondered what she was doing and whether she was with Angela or Michelle. Mostly, I wondered why she wasn't with me and how my life had come to this. Another affair. We used to tell each other our deepest thoughts and dreams, so I wondered what it was about me that caused Ken, and then Melo, to have an affair. I hoped she was just having fun with friends. Innocent hilarity.

Melo came home four days later. When she arrived, she neither smiled nor looked at me as she walked in the door. She looked around the living room. Her clothes were disheveled, like she'd slept in them. She took her backpack downstairs to the laundry and ran upstairs to the shower. I left my Spanish homework on the couch and followed her. The kids were away.

"So, where did you go?" I tried to sound nonchalant while standing in the bathroom while she showered.

"I already told you!" she snapped. "Angela's family cabin in Wisconsin."

In her room, she dressed in khaki pants with elastic around the ankles and a white T-shirt, a pile of clothes surrounding her.

"But you didn't tell me specifically where you were going."

"Yes, I did," I followed her downstairs.

"Yeah, Spooner!" I yelled. "Where is that?" She did not answer. I lowered my voice. "Melo! We've never been apart. I know this can happen, but why didn't you give me more information? I was worried. I had no phone number. Nothing."

She stopped and looked straight at me. "Worried about what?"

"I don't know. Like, who you were with. Now, where are you going?"

"Work."

"Melo, what happened with you and Angela?" Melo looked mad and focused on the floor. She was frowning, something I rarely saw her do.

After a few seconds of silence, she left to work a night shift. Her work number was constantly busy; I knew that I was absent from her heart.

Chapter 31

Melo came home later the next day. She must have gone somewhere after work. She asked me if I would come to a session with the counselor she had been seeing. I agreed and was very hopeful at the thought of having mediation in our lives: someone who could help us work out our problems, someone who would take the load off and take the jealousies away, saving me from feeling more pain. She suggested that we drive separately; she said that she had to meet alone with her counselor first, and then they would invite me into the session. I agreed, even though I felt I would be at a disadvantage because her counselor would not know me as well.

I got to the Lutheran Social Services building. There was a big, tall wall of windows on one side. There was no one in the waiting room, just an ashtray on a pedestal. I started praying for my life.

Dear Lord Jesus, please heal this relationship. Please bring us back together like we used to be. I surrender to you, Jesus. Intervene in our lives!

Melo came to the lobby from her counselor's office.

"OK, Mare," she said in a soft voice.

Walking alongside her, I was aware of the physical closeness that I had not felt for a while. Her outdoor aroma was absent. We walked silently down the gray hallway. The energy between us was vibrating in my chest. Her red-and-black high-tops were in my lateral view, untied and scuffling with each step. She opened the door for me, but she was still focused on the linoleum floor.

Her counselor was sitting behind a desk and looking very solemn. She had ear-length wavy light-brown hair and wore no makeup. I wondered if

I knew her from somewhere. She raised her chin ever so slightly when our eyes met.

The room was large and square. Melo walked to a big comfortable chair in front of the huge desk. That must have been where she sat while being counseled. There was a small, uncomfortable chair—or maybe I just felt uncomfortable—near the door. I sat down feeling anxious and hoping for a miracle.

"Hi, I'm Lois."

I held my shaking knees tight. All the windows on one side of the spacious room looked out to a back garden. Remnants of flowers stood in their dried form.

Lois leaned forward.

"For both of you, your honesty and bravery at this moment will get you through this next phase of your relationship." She took a deep breath and continued. "Mary Beth, Melo has something to say to you."

Melo faced me in her chair, one arm on the desk, the other in her lap, almost as if she had practiced. She blurted, "Mare, I have to break up with you because I had sex with Angela." Her long lashes that I adored looked downward, and her face and neck turned red. Lois just blinked, stone faced.

I stared hard at her; heat rose deep within me. The steel desk seemed longer. I let out a guttural, "No, no! Please Melo, you can't leave me, I can't live without you!" Melo sat in the same position. She was beginning to cry. "Melo, sex with Angela? What? Melo, how could you? I don't get it. What about us?"

I sobbed uncontrollably. Lois waited for me to recover before she continued.

My body folded over. Lois looked upset, and Melo cried but did not budge. Lois was excruciatingly silent. I raised my head and wiped my eyes with my sleeve. Sniffling, I darted my eyes from one to the other.

"But, but can't we do something?" I pleaded, "Can't we work it out somehow?"

I knew deep down that we were done. She had crossed a line—my line. The dried perennials outside the window darkened with the winter-solstice light. I grasped for any sign of hope. My shoulders heaved. I concentrated on the edge of Lois's desk. Lois looked at Melo.

"Mare, we can't work it out. I will be getting all my things out of the house by tomorrow." Melo glanced back at her counselor and then at me.

"No, Melo, no."

Melo handed me the box of tissues. I wanted her, not that stupid box!

I yearned for her to come across the room, comfort me, and hold me. But she did not. She sat there crying silently and wiping her now-red nose.

I was confused. We had always talked about being together forever and how no one could take our love away. Our yellow star right in the middle of Orion's Belt had been there for millions of years and would not be going any-where for another million. That is how long we were supposed to love each other. Now I did not even know her. The betrayal stung. It was like something had taken hold of her and made her not want me. We had been loving each other with the yellow star holding us together for six years—in Barrington when I met her, during the two years of divorce in Minneapolis, and then when she came to live with me these past three years. She'd always wanted me and pursued me. She had not told me she loved me for months, nor had we made love for quite a while, but I counted on that yellow-star promise.

Finally, I quieted down with a pile of crumpled tissues in my lap. The counselor wrinkled her forehead. "This has been hard for Melo and you, Mary Beth." She looked at both of us. "Now, I'm going to talk just a bit fur-ther with Melo alone. Thank you for coming in." She gave me a slight smile that turned down at the edges of her mouth.

I resisted and hung on to that room, that moment, the last time she could change, or God could make a miracle happen. But nothing hap-pened. I stood up, faced Melo—her eyes brimming with tears—and I said a tiny *bye*. Melo's quivering lips turned in. I shut the door.

Wiping my eyes continuously, I walked back down that gray hallway. It was a bitterly chilly day for September. I still had so many questions about that fucking weekend at Angela's cabin. I zipped up my jacket, my head facing downward, and walked the two blocks to my car. My world had just turned upside down. I sat in my Toyota, put my head on the steer-ing wheel, and sobbed. I felt exhausted. I drove home, hoping a car would crash into mine and kill me. I walked into my once-cheerful home crushed. Still shuddering with sobs, I went up to her room to look at her things for one last time. That sweet pile of clothes, her unmade bed. Her soccer ball and a new bike.

I heard her come in the front door downstairs. I tiptoed to my room and shut the door. I put my ear to the door. She ran up the stairs, pounding up each step like someone was chasing her, and went into the shower. I could hear her muffled crying as I entered the bathroom without knocking and stood in the doorway. My voice, a pittance against my turmoil, raged. My fists pounded the air with each word: "How could you do this, Melo?" My fingers in my hair slowly stroked my head. "I thought we were forever; you know, like the yellow star." I paused and listened while she cried softly—the shower still running. Then I blurted in anger, "You owe me money! I've been supporting you and your new girlfriend!" I grasped for straws. I wanted to hurt her back. I wanted to scream my head off.

"I don't owe you money!" she said angrily as she stuck her head out of the shower curtain.

"What do I tell the kids? That you had an affair?"

"You haven't been honest about our relationship, Mary Beth, so they wouldn't understand the word!"

Ouch! She was correct there. I had not been honest, but she knew why. She knew my situation. She knew Ken. Maybe she was tired of the charade I had insisted on. Lying about our love for each other would not work for her anymore.

"This is it, Melo—I can't take you back," I warned with a scolding finger.

She just kept crying and mumbled that she would be gone by tomorrow.

"I'm giving you a bill for all the food you've eaten, the cookie ingredients you used to give cookies to your girlfriend at the cabin—I'll have a list!" I grasped for anything. I searched for a bomb to throw at her so she would hurt like I was hurting.

"Ken will love this news! Good job, Melo! You fucked us up!" I went back to my room, locked the door, and waited. I was vengeful and self-centered in my hurt.

I had to keep things together for my children. I slipped into that familiar state of coping, putting one foot in front of the other like a zombie. I put a smile on my face and got ready to pretend.

I had no place to go. My routine had to keep progressing. I went to class that night while Melo gathered her things. I was glad the kids would not see our arguing, nor her packing. But my evening class at the University of Minnesota did not halt my tears. After exiting class early, I unfolded the door of a phone booth to call Mom.

"Mom! It's Mary Beth." I turned back and forth in the booth, trying to hide my teary, red face from a passerby.

"Oh, hi, sweetheart. Don't you have a class now?"

"Mom, Melo moved out today." I bawled uncontrollably.

"Oh, honey," she said, trying to understand. But she could not, since I'd told her Melo was just a friend.

Chapter 32

The house was silent, and I was not all right. Ken had taken the children to his home for the weekend. Melo had moved out to live with a woman from work. I was alone with bloodshot eyes.

The green IBM typewriter and Wite Out sat on the dining room table. Through the window, I saw the tops of the trees shaking in the cold wind. I shuffled through my notes, put paper in the typewriter, and began my thesis on reading in a second language. I smoked a lot of cigarettes. I could not eat. My stiff neck reminded me to stretch, so I lay on the wood floor and lifted my legs. Instead of stretching, I rolled over and cried silently. I wanted to sleep the day away. Crying exhausted me. I got up off the floor, sat back at the table, and wrote all day.

Evening came. I fed the cats. When I mounted the stairs to my room, my shoes felt like they were loaded with lead. The cold house was dark as I slumped onto my bed. My jeans and white sweater from the previous day were on the floor. A framed picture of Melo and me was propped on my nightstand. We were smiling with our arms around each other. The streetlights came on.

Wait! I thought. *I have one of her friend's phone numbers.* I called. No one answered.

"This is Mary Beth, Melo's friend. I am trying to get ahold of her because . . . because she left something here. I thought she was staying with you. Thanks. Bye." The message machine beeped.

How dumb, I did not leave a number. I was not going to call again. I was already embarrassed for making that first call. "Oh, Melo!" I said out loud to the ceiling of the empty house. "You left me. I still can't believe it!" I stomped down the hall to her room.

I leaned against the doorway and examined what was left. It still smelled like her– candy and sneakers with dried mud. I looked at her empty drawers and mattress. There were no kids running around, and I thought, *Why don't I just leave too?* My deliberations digressed; I slid downhill from working on my paper all day to wanting to disappear. As I shuffled back to my bedroom, I considered my options.

Why don't I leave forever? I fell onto my bed. *I don't think I can live anymore without her. This is it. I'm lost without her. Ken will take care of the kids. I know they'll miss me, and this will hurt them, but I just can't go on.* I started crying when I thought of them. I didn't want to go look in their rooms; doing so might make me change my mind. *Oh, my precious babies!* I faltered.

Pills were the only way I knew to end my life. I checked the medicine cabinet, and I picked up two bottles, a big one of aspirin and a small one of Advil. *Which one would kill?* I was not sure. *And how many?*

She was my savior. She helped me to rely not on others but on my strength and independence. I knew I was not Melo's savior, because she was gone. I had always had someone to lean on. Living without an arm to hang on to seemed impossible. I had to leave this impossible situation! Dying felt like my only option. Nineteen years before, Ken had been a savior when he introduced me to Jesus in a more personal way. I knew that Jesus was the only one who would never leave me.

I descended the stairs, stepped out the front door, and looked up and down the street. Alongside the wooden highway fence, Second Avenue was deserted. I wished for Melo's car. Instead, there was just the sea of cars on 35W that I could hear over the fence. I did not like that sound anymore. It no longer sounded like the ocean as I had told myself when Melo and I first rented this house together.

The silence got to me.

The bottles on my dresser clinked together. *Can I do it?* I didn't think so. *But living?* I couldn't do that either. I needed to escape. In the dark, I lay there staring at the ceiling, watching the car lights flicker from the highway.

I thought of calling someone. *Not Mom. Debra? No. Melo, Melo, where are you? What are you doing now? We had such wonderful love. What happened? You are gone. I want to just go to sleep and not wake up.*

There was no sound from the phone.

I started wailing. I did not want to be without my children. I couldn't do it. How could I leave the situation? I could not live without Melo, my savior, my fun, my friend and lover, the one who lifted me and gave me hope.

To me, Melo represented independence and freedom. She had bought a motorcycle and a windsurfer. She had done so many things I wouldn't have dared to do.

She adored me. No one has ever adored me. She followed me to Minneapolis from the East Coast. She stood up to Ken just for me when I could not. She told the truth for me when I did not. She loved me when I could not love myself. Now I had to do the challenging work and love myself. Maybe she didn't love me anymore because I didn't love myself. I wondered if my not loving myself was visible to others.

She did things spontaneously. She bought toys for herself and for the kids. She took trips to amusement parks. She would try new things and jobs, anything that paid something. It did not have to be a career or a job with prestige.

Sitting on my unmade bed, in my baggy jeans and wool socks, next to the bottles on the dresser, I contemplated how I didn't love myself. Smoking didn't help. My throat was sore from smoking so much. I lit another. My cigarette hand trembled in the dark. I pulled out the heavy phone book from the nightstand drawer. My heart pounded as I turned on the light next to me. I looked at the bottles, bottles that would give me relief; then I looked at that picture of Melo with her arms around me.

"Let's see, helpline. Oh, here in the front." My finger pointed to the number while I dialed. Someone answered right away. "I'm thinking of killing myself."

"Where are you right now?" He sounded matter of fact.

"In my bed next to a bottle of pills." I bit the cuticle on my finger.

"What's happening in your life?" he asked in a sharp voice.

I wasn't willing to tell a stranger about Melo. "I have nothing to live for."

"Is anyone there with you?"

"My kids are gone for the weekend. It would be so easy."

"But your children would come home and see you dead. Do you want that?"

I hung up without saying goodbye, sprawled on the bed, and fell asleep.

The next morning, Melo was still gone. I listened to the empty house. All I had now were my precious children. They were my reason to live.

I had nothing to lose and wanted to be truthful for the first time. There was no need to hide my love for her anymore; she was gone. I had no desire to pretend. I was not afraid of Ken anymore; he had less power over me with her gone. I would have to deal with people not liking me. That used to be important, but it was not anymore. I no longer needed to own a fancy colonial or impress college presidents. Before, when Melo was by my side, I had to protect her and hope that no one would take her away. There was nothing left to protect.

Get a grip, Mary Beth. Of course, she went for Angela. You have been hiding your true self from your kids, your family, and your friends. You have not given Melo the status of being your partner and lover. You have felt scared of being yourself and of letting down the pretenses with Melo. She has cried over you not coming out when you were with others. The damage is already done. You have not fully given yourself to her. You have tried to hide your thoughts and desires from Ken. He's no longer a threat. What have you learned?

First of all, I learned nothing was permanent except God. *She* would never leave me. Maybe I should have stopped trying to be someone else and should have just loved myself, and lavished on self-care.

I wrote in my journal for the rest of the day—Cruisie, Paul's cat, slept on my lap purring. With pen and paper, I sat in the living room and worked through my fears of coming out. Something changed with Melo's presence gone. I wrote out my prayers. I also let God tell me how valuable I was, something I used to do when I felt depressed in my marriage.

"Mary Beth, focus on Me, surrender to Me, the big details as well as the little details. Be calm. I love you—you are most important to me. I have a plan for you."

My breathing slowed down.

Then I got up, went to the kitchen, and microwaved a frozen chicken cordon bleu.

Chapter 33

I survived that dark weekend and signed up for a support group that dealt with lesbian issues and adult children of alcoholics.

My three children gathered in the living room on the white couch with tiny flowers. I nervously began my announcement.

"What, Mom? Why do we three have to all sit together?" Chris asked with a frown as he elbowed Paul.

"I have something important to tell you, sweetheart." Silence. I nervously picked a fuzzball from my sweater. "As you might have noticed, Melo hasn't been around this week."

"Where is she, Mom?" Paul asked.

"She moved in with someone else." I took a deep breath, making sure my eyes didn't water.

"Are we going to see her again?"

"You might." They were quiet. "I want you to know that I'm saying, finally, that I'm a lesbian."

Gabrielle's eyes widened, Chris smiled, and Paul furrowed his brow.

"What! What about all the times you said you weren't?" Gabrielle shouted.

"I know, honey. That was wrong." I couldn't say that I had lied. I felt I had my reasons.

"You're gay!" she yelled again. Her rosacea-ridden cheeks shone.

"Yes." I looked her straight in the eye.

"You just ruined my life!"

Chris jumped up. "I told you so! We knew you were in love with Melo, right, Paul?" Chris turned to Paul, who looked confused.

"You're still my mom, right?" He looked up with his brows lifting.

I drew Paul close. "Nothing will ever change that, sweetheart."

"Dad was right!" Chris yelled and shot up again with his arms wide open like an announcer. I tried to focus just on them and not respond to "Ken" outbursts like I usually did. He looked for my reaction. I nodded.

"Are we done yet? Can we go play now?" Chris asked.

"No," I said with a smile and a heave of air.

"What now?" Gabrielle asked. "Nick is coming soon to pick me up, and I'm late."

I pointed at her. "This will only take a minute." I was irritated that everything was always about her. This was my moment.

"I am changing my last name back to Spray." All three sets of eyes looked at me from the couch, taking it in for a few seconds.

"That's Grandma's name," Chris pointed out as he tried to understand what I was saying.

"When I was a little girl and a young woman before I married your dad, it was my name."

Paul moved to the edge of the couch. "But you're still my mom, right?"

I held my arms out. "Come 'ere, Paul." He turned. I held him on my lap and kissed his cheek with a loud sucking sound until he pulled away. "You are my son, Paul, and I will never stop being your mom no matter what you or anyone else calls me. OK?"

Chris piped up, "Can I change my name too?"

"You can when you're older, honey."

"Dad's not going to like it."

Anger hit me hard, but I relaxed my jaw and said calmly, "Chris, what I do is none of his business."

That announcement was not as hard as I had thought it would be. Telling the truth was easy, and I was not afraid of Ken anymore. I should have come out earlier. I felt better. It was an amazing feeling. A weight had been lifted. I felt free of layers of shame and self-deprecation. The kids were fine with the news. They would survive.

I stood up and got my jacket off the coat tree. "I'll be back in about an hour. I'm going to the courthouse." I backed out of the long driveway and headed down 35W. Ever since Jane, a coworker at the adoption office, had changed her name, I had been thinking about doing the same. I'd thought long and hard for a few months. Changing my name back to my birth name felt powerful. I'd saved my birthday money from Mom. Instead of buying groceries with that money, this was going to be my treat. One of the first things I did to love myself.

Sitting in the courtroom with my packet of IDs—my passport, driver's license, Social Security card, and latest tax return—I waited only a few minutes. The form wanted all my past names. They already had my former names but needed to confirm. When called, I stood up and approached a table.

"Why are you changing your name?"

"Your honor, I'm divorced and it's time."

"Are you trying to cover any past felonies?"

"No sir."

"Hand in your form and ID, please."

Why didn't I think of this before? I smiled to myself. I walked out of the Government Center feeling proud. On the way to the car, I inhaled the apple blossoms in the Minnesota spring air.

Chapter 34

Back from the courthouse with my birth name intact and my ID papers in hand, I sat down quietly to study. The kids barely noticed me. But I had a new name.

"Bam!"

"I got you with my laser beam!"

"No, you didn't! You can't kill me. I'm Darth Vader!"

I rubbed the smooth banister at the bottom of the stairs and yelled, "OK, you guys. Not so loud! I'm studying."

I heard Chris's footsteps as he ran up to his attic room. I returned to my homework.

My French dictionary and lexicon of sixteenth-century France were strewn all over the dining room table along with Rabelais's *Pantagruel*. The French lit class stressed me out. The vernacular was in old French, but my plan to integrate movement into my paper excited me: "*La Pantomime de Pantagruel: la chorégraphie de l'espace en chapitre XIX.*" The class was difficult, and I didn't understand the book, but I found a chapter where I could use movement and French ballet terms. I settled down in front of the typewriter. I only had two hours before going to the grocery store with my twenty dollars in coupons. I wanted to make those brownies Paul liked so much. They seemed to have disappeared more quickly than usual.

Eventually, I'd get a B+ on that paper. The grade thrilled me and told me I was smarter than I thought.

I noticed Gabrielle emerging frequently from the bathroom upstairs. Her eyes followed the floor in front of her footsteps. Her beautiful long, dark, curly hair poofed up on top and whiffed to the side in the day's style.

"Honey?" I paused, then cleared my throat. "How are you doing with— with what I talked about earlier . . . my being gay?" That was only the second time I had referred to myself as gay in front of her.

She ignored my question, turning her red face away.

"Mom, why did you marry Dad? You could have had someone else, anyone else." Her hand brushed over the pimples on her chin.

I led her to the living room couch, then threw my legs over the arm of the chair. She rolled her eyes at my unshaven calves.

"At that time, Gabrielle, I only saw him. I had tunnel vision. I thought only he could make me happy, even more so than Jesus! I thought that being born again would take all my problems away. I wasn't very mature then, sweetheart. Plus, I wouldn't have had you and your brothers, would I?" I surveyed her eyes and puffy face. I could hear the boys fighting again upstairs and sighed.

She twisted to pet the cat sitting in the sun on the couch and listened with her back turned. I continued, grabbing the opportunity to explain the little that I understood so far.

"Just as I came back from my year in Paris, he swooped back in my life, reestablished Jesus as my priority, and kissed me, and then I went back to college. I was twenty-one and infatuated. I redid that one kiss in my head for months." Gabrielle covered her mouth as she smiled at me. "I fell for the idea of him–someone who would take care of me. He was four years older. He led me to Christ and changed my direction in life from a young woman interested in dating and going out with friends to a young woman dedicated to the Bible first." I loosened the laces on my black high-top Doc Martens. "Grandma and Debra thought he was a phony–they saw through him. And Ginny said she could not work for him anymore, that he was too pompous and controlling. We dated mostly over the phone for six months until he proposed."

Gabrielle averted her eyes. "That's not very long, Mom." She swiveled to face me, her rosacea-reddened cheeks flaming. I was going to have to take her to the dermatologist. Behind her, the sun shone through the stained-glass windows in a kaleidoscope of colors on the worn hardwood floors. The sun highlighted the dust on the windowsill.

"I know it wasn't long." My eyes opened big. "But I was totally into him, the way he held the Bible, the way he talked about Jesus." She rotated to look at me.

"I was not ready to marry anyone then. I even had other boyfriends back in Winona! Innocently, I fell into what some women did then. I got the 'MRS' degree right after college." I quoted with my fingers. "Also, since he was a 'man of God,' I figured he was a win-win as far as happiness in marriage and thereafter. That was my big mistake, Gabrielle." I nodded, hoping she would take heed. She shifted a bit closer.

"Now, honey, I need to stand on my own with no one to lean on—not your dad, not Melo. I've been looking for a decent teaching job so I can provide more than this for you." My head circled the room.

The phone rang. She ran off, then returned shortly and sat down on the couch again.

"Mom, Nick asked me to homecoming, and I need a dress," she said in a louder voice as she moved to the edge of the couch with her hands folded primly.

"What about your friends? Do they have one you could borrow?"

She wrinkled her forehead. "Well, maybe if I lose some weight, I could borrow from Rachel."

"Can I help you to lose weight? Would you like to run with Debra and me a couple times a week?"

"I don't have time, Mom. I'm dealing with it on my own."

I got up to walk to the kitchen. I opened the harvest-green fridge door. The door stayed open because of the slanted floor. "I'm buying more salad fixings for you and me the next time I go to the store. It'll be fun!" She didn't seem interested.

"Once I get a better teaching position, I can buy better food. I'm taking one step at a time to improve my situation. For one thing, I joined an ACA group." We sauntered back to the living room.

"What's an ACA group?"

I smiled because she was listening. "It's a group of women–"

"Lesbians?" she interrupted sharply with a mocking thrust of the head.

"Yes, women like me who struggle with relationships, with finances, possibly who come from alcoholic families and feel shame. Women who are trying to find their way."

She sank back down onto the couch and pulled her cat next to her.

My voice cracked. "I don't know what the future will bring, Gabrielle. I am going to take care of you and the boys–*that* I know for sure. And yes, I am going to learn how to take care of myself too."

She smiled.

"I think I'll be fine, honey." I wiped my eyes.

"Is Melo going to appear again in our lives and make a commotion?" Her arms folded.

"No, honey, that's done. I don't even know where she is."

Her face darkened. "So now you won't wear makeup or shave under your arms?" she quipped while walking upstairs. The cat followed right behind her.

Since Melo, I had stopped wearing makeup and shaving, and I'd even let my eyebrows grow out. I loved not shaving, but my thick, dark leg hair might have been too much for her.

I knew it was going to take some time for her and the boys to accept my new lifestyle.

"Gabrielle!" I yelled from my chair.

"I just want a normal life!" I heard a door slam and then the toilet flush. I wasn't sure how to help her understand. I had just recently begun to figure out who I was myself. I missed Melo. She would have had an idea for how to approach Gabrielle.

The next task was to start my batch of Paul's favorite brownies. The recipe called for a cup of coffee in the mixture. It was under "C" for chocolate in my metal recipe box. I reached up in the cupboard for the chocolate chips and cocoa powder. The chocolate chip bag was open.

At Gabrielle's age, I too had wanted a normal family. Doors had slammed often in my family's Pierre house. During my growing-up years, my family hid painful truths with smiles on the five-minute ride to church. Mom and Dad each lit a cigarette for the short ride. We wore Mom's handmade church bonnets with long finger curls hanging down on either side of our heads like twisted tendrils on a lamp. Plastic red hat barrettes snapped at our temple to make us look like a happy family. We all wore white gloves, and the boys wore ties. But I did not identify my feelings growing up. The pain from Mom and Dad's arguments kept me silent and wanting to please them and make them happy. Every Sunday we took a whole pew. The bulletin had Dad's name at the top of the yearly posting, with $500, the highest donation. We put on our happy faces for that whole hour. We acted lies. No one said, "Now I want all of you to pretend," before we went to church. We just did it. Performing was a natural response, an organic move like swinging our arms when we walked. We put on smiles when greeting friends or the priest. But inside my heart, I was reeling with pain. The smile was imprinted on my face and the faces of most of my family—especially Mom and Dad. It was like a choreographed performance.

But when I told Gabrielle about my true identity, the pain for her was raw. We were not going to be a normal family anymore. When I was married to Ken, I tried hard to look like a normal family; I kept our arguing hidden from my Christian friends and family. I told no one about his violence, even when I hid for a day and night, afraid, in a motel. The born-again-Christian thing already set me apart as odd. I worried that I would look even more abnormal.

I knew Gabrielle was having a challenging time accepting all the changes I'd thrown at her. She was dating Debra's son, Nick, who was two years older. I also did not realize that all the toilet-flushing and missing desserts were a sign of an eating disorder. I could tell she was self-conscious about her weight, and how I, her mother, would appear to a popular high school boy.

With the whiff of chocolate coming from the kitchen, I went back to biting the skin around my nails and looking at my pile of unopened French books, fuming about not getting child support and needing to find another job for the summer when I could not substitute teach part time.

Chapter 35

Two weeks after school ended for the kids and me—after two days of delivering phone books in Cottage Grove, a suburb I had never before visited—I ended up with a thirty-five-dollar check and wear and tear on the lift hatch of my Toyota.

Ken had sent only $200 with laments about how hard it was for him. He was supposed to give me $500 a month according to the decree. Ginny and her husband gave me $100 each month to help. They based their donation on a Bible verse about caring for the widow. Since Ken wasn't paying, they stepped in with their donation.

Next to my schoolbooks sat a pile of bills on the dining-room table. The rent was seven hundred dollars.

The property owner had called the previous month to raise it to eight hundred. I told him he couldn't because I had applied for and received public heat assistance. The state sticker under my sink said the landlord could not raise the rent for two years. Electricity was forty dollars a month. I put my head in my hands. With coupons and food stamps, I could manage the food. I did not feel embarrassed tearing off the stamps in the booklet at the checkout counter. There was never enough, so I used them sparingly. They helped so much–I had no choice. The U of M bill? It was $600 a semester per class! I couldn't support my family with a thirty-five-dollar check from delivering phone books, and there would be no more rent help from Melo.

After scouring the want ads in the Sunday newspaper for a summer job, I found the perfect work: planting flowers and digging in the dirt. I dearly wanted to get back into teaching. To make ends meet between getting a pink slip as a nontenured teacher every May and possibly getting rehired in the fall, I applied for a summer job at a landscaping company. It paid seven dollars per hour. That, plus public health care, helped me financially.

Dressed in rolled-up cutoffs, a T-shirt, and steel-toe hand-me-down boots, I showed up to work for Todd and Brad, a gay couple. Five men lived in their house, a mansion on Emerson in the upscale Lowry Hill neighborhood. Each room was decorated, from the hand-painted crown molding on the ceiling to the chandeliers. They had extravagant window coverings and a meticulous garden with *Coreopsis* moonbeam cleverly positioned in even rows.

In the morning, we met in their kitchen. Brad offered me and two other workers a coffee. Brad was short, husky, and slightly balding. He wore glasses. Todd had a gut and thick graying hair hanging over his forehead.

"Today, we're planting pygmy barberry bushes and laying cement sidewalks. Mary Beth"—he swallowed—"will you gather the shovels, rakes, and bags of cement?"

"Yes." I saluted him in a playful mood, happy to be employed for the summer. Gabrielle babysat the boys, who were eleven and eight years old. When she went to work, she had to find a sitter amongst her friends. I found out later that my two older kids harassed Paul, my youngest, to tears. Chris bullied Paul, and I was not on top of it.

Brad, Todd, and I hopped in the red F-150 and met the others at the worksite. The earthy bouquet was intoxicating as I thrust my pointy shovel into the crumbly dirt Todd had marked for me on landscape fabric.

"No, Mary Beth, like this." Todd took my shovel and showed me how to line it up perfectly. They were both patient with me. I learned.

Soon it rained, and the shoveling became backbreaking. I emptied the whole truck bed of muddy dirt. They never canceled when it rained, except for cement jobs. Still, it was fun working for them. Brad often brought up politics.

"But we still have plenty to do with gay rights, employment issues–" He started counting on his fingers.

"And custody issues," I piped up.

He turned to me. "You know, Mary Beth, you can contact the Minnesota Civil Liberties Union?"

The idea that Ken might try to take my kids loomed in my head. But I had no intention of contacting the MCLU, because gay people did not have the same rights as heterosexuals. My priorities were to put food on the table and raise three children.

In the late eighties, my politics progressively shifted from the conservative slant Ken and my parents had previously endorsed. Growing up, I was proud of my family's views and was told that the "commies" and "pinkos" would try to change my mind. Over the years, my views gradually reversed. In the early seventies, when I sat in front of the college TV every day and watched the names of five to ten men my age who had been killed that day, I reversed my view on not protesting the Vietnam War. But my shifting politics remained unspoken, a secret kept only by me.

As a single parent, I needed financial welfare help. As a bisexual, I felt the hate of a man putting a Bible in front of my face and saying, "Jesus can save you." Most of all, I have been appalled up to the present day at how evangelicals have used their religion to judge and ignore others, the complete opposite of what the Bible instructs.

After work, I came home trudging up each step. My body hurt, my arms and hands barely moved, and my back ached. I went upstairs, kicked off my boots, and rested for a half hour. The boys knew that I was not to be disturbed. At age fourteen, Gabrielle usually worked at the nearby Cathay Chow Mein during dinner and hung out with Nick as much as possible before and after.

"Mom!" Gabrielle rushed in after walking the three blocks home across the 35W overpass. "My boss makes me add up all the orders by hand. No calculators." Her purse dropped by the front door, and her arms opened in supplication. "She called me a stupid girl!"

I raised one eyebrow with a smile, my wooden spoon in hand, dripping tomato sauce. "Then your math will improve, and you can ignore her put-downs." She rolled her eyes as she ran up the stairs, two at a time, taking her ponytail out.

"I'm going out with Nick in twenty minutes. I have to shower and get this deep-fried smell off me."

"I have taco pie!" I shouted from the kitchen.

"I ate at work!" she yelled from upstairs.

Paul ran down the stairs, a big, toothy smile on his nine-year-old face. "I smell taco pie, Mom." His front teeth were parting. I knew I'd have to look into braces. I was going to have to mention it to Ken. He oversaw the kids' health care on his wife's insurance.

"Did I hear taco pie?" Chris came in from outside.

"Let's sit down. Who wants to pray?"

"Not me," Chris said.

"Not me," Paul imitated his brother.

"OK. *Dear Jesus, thank you for this yummy food and for this house to live in. Amen.*"

"Mom?" Paul started whining. "Chris is always teasing me."

"Chris, what are you doing to him?" I asked as I lifted a Dorito chip full of ground beef and cheese with my fingers.

"Nothing."

Sitting down finally reminded me that I was exhausted. I forgot to pursue Chris's teasing.

Chapter 36

Maintaining a social life was draining as a single mom. When the kids visited Ken, I needed to get out. Being single in the gay nightlife had a different veneer than when Melo and I had danced the evenings away together.

I looked straight with my long hair and matching green cords and silk blouse. Sitting by myself at a tiny round table one night at Ladies' Night was tough; I felt lonely. No one danced. Maybe 9:00 p.m. was too early. I looked around, keeping an eye out for loud, fun-loving Melo. But she was missing. And there was no replica of her either. I was not sure what I would have done if she had appeared, because I still missed her. It had been over three months since we broke up. Only once had I called her and hung up.

A woman approached me from behind.

"Hi, can I sit down?"

I gestured to the chair. She had short light-brown hair. Her tall frame was not like Melo's. (I still compared every woman to Melo.) She wore ironed jeans and a button-down with the collar up. We danced. She did not know how to dance to "Jump"; she had none of Melo's energy. I imitated her minimalist moves, waving my arms back and forth to the music. No fancy Michael Jackson moves like I used to do. I did not feel the music. When we slow danced to "Nothing Compares 2 U," I noticed her hand shifting along my back. I forced my head back to keep from touching her cheek. After the song ended, we grabbed our chairs. They scraped on the dark, rubbery painted floor.

"Some friends and I are having a small party tonight in Maplewood. Would you like to join us?" I didn't, really, but I was companionless and hoped it might be fun. I told myself I could meet some cool women.

"Well, maybe, but Maplewood? Isn't that kind of far?"

She leaned forward on her elbows. "I'll drive you and then bring you back to your car." Her smile was bright on an otherwise forgettable face. I thought about it and looked at my watch: 10:00 p.m. already. It would be a late night, but my loneliness made the choice.

"OK."

She drove me, and it seemed far away. I was doubting my decision. She made small talk and looked at me a lot as she drove. A forty-five-minute ride to party with people I did not know, then forty-five minutes back to my car, after which I'd still have to drive home . . . I looked out the window into the night and tapped my fingers on the car door as we drove to a suburb I knew little about.

We entered a rambler house. It was so sparsely furnished, it almost looked like a meeting place instead of a place where someone lived. A balding, ordinary-looking man surveyed me from across the expansive living room. He sat in a chair, and a woman stood behind him. He talked quietly with her.

"These are my friends." Her hand swooped in their direction.

"Hi." That was all I could muster. My stomach turned. I chose a spot on the couch, keeping my jacket on. It looked like a small party to me.

"Let me take your coat." She smiled at me with her hand out, but my stone face remained. "Would you like some pot?"

I was startled at the question. "No!"

The man and woman grinned at each other.

"A drink, then?"

I slid to the edge of the big green-and-brown flowered couch while she prepared a rum and Coke. The house smelled dusty.

She came back from a dimly lit kitchen, glass in hand, and set the drink on the shiny wooden end table. Rings of watermarks lined the spot where she set the drink. As she settled in without speaking, her arms surrounded me from behind. She smelled like Eternity perfume. My heart pounded. The man came and put his arms around her and the other woman around him. We were in a line. She started kissing my neck. It felt wet like she was licking me.

"No!" I said again. I wriggled out of her embrace. They continued kissing one another. I turned my back on them and looked out the curtainless dark window. I saw nothing. I was stranded with no way to get home, and I did not even know where I was.

"We're going in the bedroom. Do you want to join us?"

"No, thank you."

They all left. As I sat alone in the dark living room, I could hear one woman yell out in orgasm, then another. I waited for noise from the man but heard nothing. *How long am I going to be here? How did I stupidly get myself into this creepy situation?* I began to berate myself. After waiting and pacing for an hour, I wondered how I could leave on my own with less than ten dollars in my pocket. I prayed to leave that place safely. She finally came out of the bedroom.

"I'd like to go home."

"Sure, I'll take you." I put my double-breasted polyester jacket on. "Home, or to your car?"

"My car."

She drove back to Ladies' Night. She tried to kiss me, but I turned my face.

The familiar smell of my car calmed my shivering. Soon I was on 35W and heading toward the Diamond Lake Road exit. I was happy to be home and very much alone. Before I snuggled into my bed, I picked up the phone and dialed Melo's number just to hear her voice. The ringing went on for a long time; I hung up.

I decided to dedicate myself solely to parenting and my master's homework. Besides, my Adult Children of Alcoholics group was starting back up soon, and I knew I could meet women there.

Chapter 37

The following day, I took a deep breath and looked up the stairs to the ACA meeting. We arranged ourselves in a crowded circle on gray Berber carpet squares in the upstairs room. Only one chair was empty. Some of the women smiled; others looked angry, with knitted foreheads. Although eager to meet these women, I sat quietly, maybe squeaking out a "hi" if someone addressed me.

The leader of the group was a woman who had been with her partner for twenty years. That floored me; I wanted to trust her and felt respect for her. She must have been in her forties, just a few years older than me. Her chair was under the only window. There were a few books on the shelf behind her.

"Welcome." She slowly looked around the room at each of us, her brown hair parted down the side with bits of gray. She had a double chin. "We're going to do some work in this group and dig deep into the family we didn't choose–those who emotionally abandoned us while growing up. All of us have three things in common: we are identifying as lesbians; we grew up in an alcoholic family; and because of that, we have chosen violent relationships of several kinds." She paused and directed her eyes at each of us again. "Is that correct?" There were a few nods.

"Can I smoke?" The woman who asked had a shaved fade up the back of her head. Her teeth were gray. "I may need a break if things get heavy."

"No smoking. Sorry."

This wasn't my first ACA meeting. The conversation in that group hit me hard. They talked about how the oldest child of an alcoholic was a pleaser and rule follower. They mentioned how blame was used in the family and how every child developed a keen sense of reading others.

But this one was specifically for gay women. I was proud and excited to be identifying as a lesbian. I felt that breaking up with Melo had helped me see myself. This was a new way of thinking for me, because I had been closeted when Melo lived with us.

We went around the circle and shared a bit of the pain in our lives from growing up in a dysfunctional family.

One woman instantly caught my eye after she chugged up the stairs to our meeting room in her steel-toed boots. She untied the laces and stole a few minutes of our precious meeting. We all sat in silence watching her until the leader eventually asked her to introduce herself. As she lifted her red-wool-stockinged feet out of her footwear, her black ponytail and boots took my breath away.

Upending her shoe like she was shaking something out, she said, "Sorry I'm late, I just got off work." Then she set her boot next to the other one in the middle of our circle. She looked at us and shared. "My lover, her daughter, and I are living together, but things aren't going too well. My sister and I are both dykes. I hate my stepdad and brother. They're violent to my sister and mom." She leaned back and folded her arms. Her long jean-covered legs stretched straight out into the center of the circle.

I could see that my turn was next. I was trembling. "I'm here because I broke up with my girlfriend"—it was my first time calling her that—"and I'm lost." I kept my eyes downward. "I was pretty much lost growing up in my family too." It felt good to speak that last sentence. I emptied some childhood baggage and proclaimed a truth. I was relieved.

The leader drew our attention back to her and handed out sheets of paper to each of us. "I want to talk about a few organizations that might help you from time to time—a writers' group, a social group, and a list of gay-friendly churches. If you're single or not, it's a nice way to make connections."

The leader turned to me.

"So, Mary Beth, tell us a story about growing up in your family."

Heat rose in my face. My mind went to the small two-bedroom house north of the South Dakota capitol building.

"My parents screamed at each other all the time. I saw my dad hit my mom when I was little."

The leader leaned in. "Can you tell us about that time, Mary Beth?" I sat for a few seconds, then cleared my throat.

"I was four and heard loud voices in the kitchen. I remember I couldn't see my mom's face at first. I yelled for her as I sat obediently in the living room in front of the giant window of our new house. My body jumped at the sound of a slap, and then I heard soft weeping. It was her sobbing that grounded me. Someone I loved was being hurt by someone else I loved. I couldn't see past the rounded shoulders of the Frigidaire. Sitting on the edge of the davenport, I could not control my tears. Dad appeared at my side; he knelt eye to eye and said he was sorry, that he'd never do it again, while wiping my face with his ironed cloth hankie."

I took a breath and looked around–everyone stared at me as if they were trying hard to imagine my scene. The room was quiet. The clock on the wall showed we had only fifteen minutes left.

"Sounds awful, Mary Beth," the leader said to me.

"I felt that something was wrong with me—that maybe if I did the right thing, I could make my parents happy, and the screaming would go away. I thought I was bad and that their pain was my fault. I still do sometimes." I could feel my tears rising uncontrollably. "Shame is still flourishing in my life." I wiped my eyes. Some of the group members leaned forward in their folding chairs.

"Then I"—putting my hand to my chest—"married an asshole who did the same thing!" One woman inhaled forcefully. I hoped I had not said too much in front of these women I did not know. Usually, I questioned myself when I gave an opinion. *Will they think I'm dumb?* On the other hand, I felt freedom about talking with women who had similar issues.

A couple of the participants teared up. The tissue box was passed around.

"Who else is dealing with some kind of shame?" The leader looked around the room. Hands went up, and some nodded. There was not a lot of eye contact.

Surrounded by concerned women, I side glanced at the dark-haired woman, Char. Her brows were drawn together. I felt a twinge and thought of how Melo used to care for me. Maybe Char could take me in her arms and give me attention as Melo once had.

Chapter 38

Months went by while I attended the weekly group, continued taking classes, and substitute taught. The kids went to school and hung out with friends. Melo rarely came to mind. One rainy March Saturday evening, I drudged over my *Managing Problem Behaviors* book from the U. I sat at the dining room table and imagined myself in front of my students. *Hopefully, when I have finished this master's program, I will have that classroom and a few behaviors to manage; I would take any behavior!*

The doorbell rang. I turned off the old copper-colored lamp with the twisted neck and walked into the shadows to answer the door.

There stood Melo.

I had an instant pang in my chest. Looking beyond her for a second, I noticed the blue Mustang was parked in front. Her hand touched the door frame; her eyes glanced into the house behind me. When I saw her, I burst into tears and quickly tried to dry my eyes.

She gave a quick, nervous wave.

"Hi, Mare." She bit her upper lip as her smile and her red neck greeted me along with the twilight over 35W. She wore clothes I did not recognize: white high-tops, tapered stonewashed jeans, and a black leather jacket with diagonal zippers over several pockets. Her long, muscular legs bounced like she was going to shoot a basketball.

I wiped my eyes again, surprised at my own reaction and uncertain whether I wanted to invite her in. "Hi, Melo."

"It's so dark here. No kids?" Her outdoor fragrance of asphalt entered with her and reminded me of Paris streets.

"Ken's." I sighed while twisting a corkscrew of hair around my finger. "I'm working on a paper." After clearing my throat, I looked in the direction of the dark dining room.

She stared at me and opened her arms for a hug.

I just shook my head with a lump in my throat. My whole body ached for those arms around me, but danger lights flashed inside me.

She lowered her arms and persisted. "I have something for you. A gift." She smiled as she shifted from side to side. "Can I come in?"

Every move of hers captivated me; how her voice lowered sometimes. She seemed light on her toes. The roar of an airplane directly overhead brought me back to reality. I shook my head again. "Melo, we can't." Still standing in the entryway, I pulled my permed hair into a poufy ball of a ponytail and cleared my throat again. I wanted to put my head on her chest and fall asleep.

On the other hand, I felt that I had cleared my home of Melo. I had willed her out of my life. Giving in a little, I said, "How about we meet at Perkins and talk?"

On the short drive over to Perkins, I wondered what I was doing. The last time I'd gone to Perkins was to meet Angela to ask her what had occurred that weekend at the cabin. She wouldn't tell me what had happened. In the parking lot, I wondered whether Melo was seeing Angela. *Who is she with now? Who does she laugh with and tease now?* My mind and heart had been closed to all questions these past months.

We sat by a window in Perkins. Melo swished around in her booth seat, looked in her backpack, and picked up the menu. She showed me an invention she'd made to hold a cap on a belt. Her laugh had a humming ending that went on for a couple of seconds. The server came over with her thermos of coffee, and it reminded me of when I'd sat there with Angela.

I fought back tears, picked up the Kap-Pac (her invention that she'd left on the table), and tried to look interested in it.

"No, like this." She took it from my hand and brushed my palm slightly with her fingers. I felt her electricity. She paused and took in a deep breath with the touch.

She leaned back and fiddled with the button on the red Perkins booth, avoiding eye contact. Then I mentioned Ken not paying much. "Chris is stealing my cigarettes."

She smiled. "If I were there in your—*our*—house, I'd catch him!"

I ignored her inclusion of a reference to my house. "Paul is only eight, and he worships Chris."

She nodded.

"And Gabrielle is enraptured with Nick."

"I saw that coming, Mare. You'd better keep a lookout."

Then we asked each other about dating. "But I'm meeting people. I have some new friends in an ACA group. I'm looking at some of the shitty stuff from when I grew up."

"Like what?"

Not wanting to go into detail, I said, "Oh, like feeling unimportant, low self-image, that stuff." She had a way of getting me to talk about deep feelings. I did not want to get sucked in. Even though I might have wanted more, I just could not trust her.

I switched the subject. "Are you praying or writing?"

"Not much. How about you? Still reading the Bible?"

"I have a running prayer going on inside me, but I must rethink the Bible reading because it seems so hypocritical with how Ken talked about it and then screwed me over. Not sure I trust evangelicals anymore."

The waiter came by with a coffee pot again. We sat quietly together for a long minute.

"Mare, I want to get together again." Her hands rested on the table for a moment of silence, inching their way closer to mine.

"Whoa!" I shook my head. "Melo, I–"

Her arms stretched across the table—her hands on my edge of the booth. "Just think about it, Mare! I'm sorry. I've learned my lesson." She blinked tears with those straight lashes.

I put my hands on my stomach. "We had such a complicated relationship." I heaved a big sigh. "I almost stopped breathing." Not wanting to share the details. "The kids? Our family? We had so much."

"I know, I know, Mare." Shaking her head. "I miss the kids terribly."

I ignored her statement.

She pulled a seductive dancing ceramic statue from her bag. It was all wrapped in ribbons and tissue paper: a reclining woman with one leg in a passé position.

"What do you think, Mare? I know you like it." She smiled and glanced around, not caring who saw her. It was big, and it endeared me to think of how she'd put thought into choosing it, tailor made for my love of dance and teaching ballet. I knew if I picked it up and touched it, then I would want to feel her near me. She lifted it to show me every angle. "See how she's lying on her side? I think she's dreaming about something."

Afraid that I might give in for a moment, I teetered. My insides swirled. The statue was cool, but I knew it was over.

"I can't take your gift, Melo." I thought about leaving. I was getting uncomfortable. I sat on the edge of the booth cushion holding my jacket.

"I came out to the kids, Melo." Now it was my turn to look down.

"What!" She thrust her head forward. "You're a lesbian now?"

"Shush!" I said, looking around. I was still not ready to take many risks. A few heads turned.

"Why didn't you come out when we were together?" She wrinkled her forehead between her squinting eyes. "That makes me mad, Mare." She stared at me, then took my hand. "I know why you didn't come out when I was with you. I know how hard it was for you." Her other hand moved across the table. She always tried to see my side.

"Let's get back together, Mare." Her eyes were wide and hopeful. After savoring the two-second hold, I pulled my hand away.

"No, Melo. I can't. It's done between us." I started putting my jacket on. "The sex with Angela finished it for me." I could not sit conflicted with her for another minute. "And just like Ken, you didn't talk to me about it or tell me what happened. I thought you were more honest than him." I still harbored anger. "I had to come here and meet with Angela and ask a ton of questions!" I stood up.

"But Mare!" She grabbed my jacket. "I am honest! That's why I finally told you."

"Once you left, Melo, I had nothing to lose. You broke my heart." I did not care if strangers heard me at that moment. "I finally had to come out to myself. I was too afraid to do it earlier." I took a deep breath and looked outside. "The truth felt good, Melo." All I gave her was a tiny smile.

It took everything I had to walk out of Perkins and not stop in the somber evening. I went through my front door, shut it, slid down the wall, and sobbed.

Chapter 39

I stood on the dark sidelines like in high school, dying to dance. I was too shy to get on the floor; I tried to hold down my shoulders from bursting into movement.

As a small girl, I danced to Mom's records. When alone, I would put on Teresa Brewer's "Music! Music! Music!" and Johnny Horton's "North to Alaska." The phonograph was my pal as I lifted the needle over and over to Johnny Cash's "Sixteen Tons." I interpreted Mom's records of the current musicals and danced around the living room floor in flowing dresses. I imagined myself as the main dancer. Mom said that when I was only two, I took steps and then jiggled to the music in front of the jukebox at a restaurant in Edgemont, South Dakota.

At Rumours night club, many unique men and women danced their funky moves. A woman with a shaved head (except for a few curls at the top) wiggled her behind to Paula Abdul's "Straight Up" in front of another woman in spiked heels. Handsome men in tight shirts and pants which accented their perfect physiques swing danced, taking up the dance floor. Their arms stretched out after a twirl, and their lips touched as they curled together. There was extra freedom under the glittery rotating glass disco ball that sent moving rays of light across the bodies and faces in the room. There were no judgments; no one told us we were sinners. There were no shaming looks. When "Jump" came on, dancers leaped in unison whenever they heard the word, enjoying the collective feeling of being airborne for a second. This club was a refuge.

But there was pressure. At least I felt it. The principles of asking someone to dance had switched. I could ask anyone and did not have to wait for a boy to ask me, like in the hetero world. Or I could just dance by myself. When I danced by myself, I felt powerful.

That was unheard of in conservative Pierre during the fifties and sixties. Girls could not show initiative—they had to be led to the floor.

The energy was enticing; the song "Everybody Dance Now" drew me in. Eighties dance music was an outlet for me to throw my body into another dimension for the duration of the song, to get lost far from my worries, to let my body take over. The pounding beat was what I liked the most. I didn't even listen to the words. Plus, heads turned with my dance moves.

However, that night I leaned against a table by the crowded wall, looking for Melo to appear or for a female knight-in-shining-leather to approach. I relaxed a little, even though Melo's face flashed continuously before me. I scanned the crowd. Roberta, Angela's ex, appeared out of the lighted entrance area. She was gorgeous. Her shoulder-length black hair was tucked behind her ears. A cigarette hung from her puffy lips, and she seemed slimmer than the last time I'd seen her, more fit.

"Hi, Roberta." She was already smiling big at me. Then she put her smoky breath up to my ear to talk over the music.

"How are you doing?" With her most sympathetic therapy face, she looked at me closely. She blew the smoke away from me with an upward nod. I lit one.

"I'm getting there," I lied while stuffing my gloves into my winter jacket.

"Let's dance." Grinning, I led her by her hand onto the dance floor under the sparkly revolving globe. Her dance style was more subdued than Melo's. We slow danced gingerly to "Black Velvet." I took the lead since I felt confident dancing. She laughed when I twirled her under my arm.

Her continuous smile made me grin from ear to ear. The barroom was full of smoke and drinking. The music and voices were deafening as the night went on. She bought me a rum and Coke. We stayed till the lights came on. The bright exposure took away from the night's glamour and revealed a ragged toll on the faces of the late-night dancers: makeup had drooped, and there were sweaty brows, unsteady feet, swaying bodies, some shouting, and some crying. We walked together to the back parking lot, into the quiet fresh air.

That Sunday afternoon, Roberta called. She invited me to dinner the following Saturday at seven o'clock. I still ached for Melo. My counselor at the U of M had told me directly that she thought I should not date anyone for a while, a good year. Well, that only lasted six months. I had a challenging time being alone. I felt I always had to have someone near me to tell me I was important. I hadn't yet learned to be alone with myself. Having not dated since Melo, I ignored my counselor's advice. Besides, there was so much about Roberta that intrigued me, and I noticed she was not drinking. It seemed she had her life together. I wanted to know more.

Roberta picked me up in her baby-blue MG. She wore swirly loose pants and a sports coat. She looked badass. She lit a cigarette, and we drove off. I felt excited as a teenager in that sports car. I did not say much and looked out the passenger-side window. Out of my peripheral vision, I saw her profile with a now-short cigarette hanging down from her mouth. She kept her eyes forward. On the dashboard was a single pink rose. With downward eyes, she handed it to me.

"Thank you for the rose," I said.

The sports car's motor grabbed the road smoothly. We went to the Italian restaurant Vescio's in St. Louis Park. I closed my eyes and lifted the rose to my face several times during the ride. After parking, she came around and opened my door. We sat at a single table in the smoking section. It was fun again, looking at a menu with someone new. We shared meatballs and spaghetti with a salad.

Roberta leaned forward, twisted a handful of hair, dropped it on her neck, and asked, "Have you found a teaching job yet?"

"No, just subbing. I quit a nonprofit job."

"Why did you quit?" She wrapped spaghetti around her fork.

"It didn't pay well." I cleared my throat. "And the husband of my boss was creepy."

"What?"

I looked to the couples around me conversing at their red-checkered covered tables. The hum of their conversations gave me privacy. "He put his arms around me at his office and kissed me once at a company potluck at my house–in front of his children." I slowly raised my eyes.

She set her fork down.

"I didn't like it."

"Didn't like it? Mary Beth! That's inappropriate!" Her eyes opened wide.

"Yeah." I looked at my plate. "I didn't know what to do." I still have a tough time confronting straight men. I'm sure I give them too much power in my presence.

"Mary Beth, you tell him *no* and that you'll call the cops."

My red-checkered napkin covered my mouth. "I couldn't have done that, Roberta." I shook my head. "I needed that job."

"How is it for you not to teach full time?"

"Hard." I cleared my throat.

"Have you seen her?"

"Once."

Roberta took in a deep inhale. "You know, when you're ready, MB, we can talk about that weekend."

My body quivered. I didn't dare ask her more but was curious about what she knew.

"Hey, I noticed that you weren't drinking last week, and you look great."

She nodded. "Yeah, things got crazy when I was with Angela. We drank too much."

"Did you drink with your husband that year you were married before you met Angela?" I hadn't noticed her drinking when I was still with Melo.

"Not much, so I want to go back to an even keel with alcohol."

"Sounds good, Roberta. I want to go forward to a life of fun living."

She was comforting and attentive; she seemed genuinely concerned with my welfare. My romantic life had been a barren desert since Melo left.

Roberta placed a soft kiss on my lips before I jumped out and ran up to my big four-square house. It seemed like forever since I had been kissed. I thought about Roberta that night instead of Melo.

Chapter 40

As I walked around Diamond Lake, I thought about how I was entering dangerous ground when I compared Melo to Roberta. Melo's sense of freedom had left an imprint on me. Some of my childhood pain had opened and healed with Melo. She was my first female love. My persona changed because of her. I'd made steps of self-discovery with Melo. My eyes opened to more possibilities for me as a woman. I realized how much I loved women. I loved the sound of their voices, their gentle softness. I loved their bodies. I loved breaking the old mold in my head that women were secondary to men. That thought gave me energy. Roberta seemed like another example of the woman I loved. She was financially stable and did things like owning two sports cars. She had a freedom that I still didn't have. The homes tucked in the woods around Diamond Lake let me daydream about having my own someday.

On our next dancing date, Roberta focused her attention on me. Cheek to cheek, we slow danced in our short skirts at the women's bar. If the community judged us, we were unconcerned. I had heard comments that certain kinds of clothing–like short skirts–weren't lesbian appropriate. We had been seeing each other for a couple of months. Wondering who Melo was with, I still looked in the dark shadows of Ladies' Night for her or Angela.

"Are you OK?" Roberta asked, as she loosened her arms from around me and looked me in the eye. Her dark hair swayed.

"Yeah, sort of," I answered.

She nodded, led me by my hand to a table, and came back from the bar with two drinks–not her usual coffee. That evening, I wore a T-shirt that said, "I just LOOK straight."

"You're drinking again?"

"Yup." She took a big swig of her Bacardi and Diet Coke, then lit a cigarette. "I can handle it." She fiddled with her rings.

"But you stopped these past months?"

"I just wanted to get my head straight after that mess with Angela."

I had never confronted anyone about their drinking habits. I never saw my dad drink. I did mention to Ken's dad that he was not allowed in our home when he drank. Ken and I did not drink during our thirteen years of marriage. Melo and I drank mostly on the weekends. I worried that maybe I'd made a bad choice in hanging out with Roberta.

She made plenty of money with her two jobs. As a group home director of kids separated from their families, she did everything from cooking dinner to hiring and firing. Her second job took her late into the wee hours; she answered a helpline phone for several businesses. She was very skilled at both. Maybe she was a workaholic. I knew that some alcoholics try to keep busy so they don't drink.

Maybe her drinking at the bar was a one-time deal. I hoped that things would work out with us; she listened, spent money on me, and was strong. She treated me like a princess. I could have asked for anything from her. She wasn't the same with the kids as Melo. Her style was more help orientated, not playful like Melo.

Gabrielle tried out for hockey cheerleading. The expenses of a teenager worried me. I kissed the top of her head and noticed again her blurry eyes and red cheeks. I was not spending enough time with her. She needed me. Her clothes were ill fitting; she exposed too much cleavage. I needed to step up somehow.

Roberta took me shopping at Ragstock and spent $160 on used clothes for the two of us. She even bought a few for Gabrielle. I had never seen that much spent on clothes in one day. She told me what looked good, but she smelled like booze.

Roberta skillfully draped a jean jacket over a shirt that made Gabrielle look slimmer. Gabrielle clapped as she twirled in the full-length mirror.

Occasionally, Roberta dropped in and hung out with me and the kids. The kids knew we were dating, but they had no response to me dating her. They just tolerated me, I think. She wore an apple-green fanny pack I had given her as a gift and some of the new clothes from Ragstock. Her wrists and one ear were adorned with bracelets and earrings. I liked her more as a companion to hang around with than as a girlfriend. She was attractive and attentive to me. But she didn't engage with the kids much.

After a few more months of dating, we were driving on Clinton Avenue. She brought a plastic Twins cup full of rum and Coke into my car. These drinking habits of hers were foreign to me.

"Mary Beth, I want you to look at this house I'm thinking about buying. It's right across from Morrison Park, where the kids play ball."

"Sure! I love looking at houses." *Is she purposely buying it near me?* "You know, Roberta, I'm only renting this house; I won't be here long." I looked at her plastic cup. "What if we get stopped?"

"I'll just pour it on the floor."

My eyes glanced at the car mat. "Really?" I wondered if the smell of the empty cup would give her away.

She changed the subject. "Stop here, Mary Beth—this one has five bedrooms." She stretched her hand toward a small-but-cute house with many gables and a fenced-in backyard.

"Five bedrooms! What are you going to do with five bedrooms!"

"Hopefully, I'll fill them up." She winked at me. I bit my nails. I liked her, but did not love her. She'd gone for me so fast. Amid her strengths, I saw her possible weaknesses—alcohol abuse, clinginess, needing a family. *Am I her substitute family? Even a mom figure?* Her mom had sexually abused her. Yet, she had the financial ability to take care of me. I was looking for a mom too–someone to be a caretaker—like I had when I married Ken. He'd been older, successful, and confident on the outside. He came from a family where his dad drank and hit his mom. He hit me. I did not love him deeply when we married, but I thought he would take care of me. God was his friend.

"Do you want to see the inside?" She squished the fire end of her half-smoked cigarette on the inside of the windshield and wedged the stinky butt back into her pack of Virginia Slims. I looked at the smudged spot on the window. I didn't like how she treated my car.

"We can just walk in?" I turned the car off.

"Yeah." She held up the keys. We toured the house. I "oohed" and "ah-hed" in every room. It was a two-bedroom on the main floor. The second floor was remodeled into a clever living space with three bedrooms and a huge family room with big windows that overlooked the backyard. She knew I would like it and asked her dad for help on the down payment.

After looking at a few more houses, she asked, "Which one do you like best Mary Beth? The one on Portland or the one on Clinton?"

"I like the one on Clinton, Roberta. But you have to buy it because you like it, not me."

"Mary Beth, could you ever see yourself living here?"

"Roberta, I—I don't. What are you asking? That we live together, and I bring my kids here to live? It's gorgeous and everything, and my kids would love it. But I'm not ready to make that kind of commitment. Besides–"

"Besides what?"

I turned away from her.

"What, Mary Beth?"

"You started drinking again." My hands were on my hips.

"What's wrong with that? You drink! I'm buying this house for me, Mary Beth. And I'm walking home." She slammed the car door.

She called later that evening, and I reminded her that drinking in my car was not OK. She apologized.

Her rekindled relationship with alcohol bothered me. I drank, but I did not trust her starting up again. And yet, I continued to see her but stayed on high alert.

She called me often but seldom came over between jobs. She was easy to be with, not too demanding with my busy schedule. I envied her full-time job security. I even asked her to set me up with the phone-answering job, but I didn't have the qualifications. She must have heard my comment about her drinking; she eased up in front of me.

Ken slowed down with his comments about Melo but not about my lifestyle. I thought he might be nervous that his ex-wife looked like she was rejecting men, or more specifically, that Ken had driven me to women. I'm sure the kids told Ken that I'd come out as a lesbian and was dating a new person. He was probably nervous that my being gay reflected poorly on him. His new wife had two boys; they lived with their dad. He faithfully took our kids on Wednesdays and every other weekend.

About a year after our divorce, he married his secretary. I don't think he wanted to go too long without someone to cook for him. Plus, he liked secretaries. Pauline was his secretary in Pierre. The kids said everything was clean at their dad's house and that Sandra, his wife, seemed obsessive, especially about cleanliness. I was glad he was married. I hoped it meant he would lay off harassing me. I wondered if he remarried so quickly to keep his masculine narcissistic image intact, to show people he was still wanted by someone.

Roberta drove me places in her fancy cars; we packed to camp on Madeline Island. Her two-seater cars were attractive to me. She stuffed all our tent and camping gear into the tiny trunk, obscuring the rear window. I would have prepared with maps and food, but she just packed, and we went.

Driving north, we listened to Tracy Chapman's *Matters of the Heart*. I loved the whole women's culture I was being introduced to. Songs that told of love between two women. It reminded me of when I heard cool songs for Christians. It kind of made the extremeness of evangelicals and same-sex unions mollify a bit in my mind. I could be unique and still blend in and be cool.

We leaned over the ferry railing on a summer day, surrounded by blue sky and cotton clouds. I was excited about a new adventure. "Look! I see the island."

"I have treats planned for you." She laid her head on my shoulder; the breeze blew through our hair. The lotus tattoo on her left shoulder peeked out. Her beautiful curled eyelashes covered her closed eyes. She handed me a pink plastic tube with a black speed adjuster at one end. "Your very own vibrator."

I quickly stuck it in my pocket and patted it. I love the women's world where women's desires are paramount. "That'll be fun." I tipped my head toward her. We got in the car and made out until the ferry landed.

Our campfire that evening spit sparks. We had hot dogs on sticks with ketchup. She poured the brandy and diet coke. We made s'mores. In the early morning, I could smell the coffee on the cookstove. I positioned a slice of bread on the pyramid toaster, then slathered on the butter and dunked it in my coffee. My favorite breakfast.

"Let's go for a walk in Big Bay State Park," I suggested.

"Sure—let me get something first," she said as I tied my shoes.

"I want to walk along the east side of the island and hear the waves."

"OK, I'll be right there." She was fumbling in her backpack.

The walk to the shore was not far. It was windy. I inhaled the prominent pine smell as I climbed the immense boulders. Water splashed up on my sneakers. It reminded me of Rhode Island. I still mourned the colonial home, lobsters, fresh fish, foghorns of ships, and the exotic dream life I wanted living by an ocean.

I sat down on a flat stone, lit a cigarette, and soaked in the sun on my face and body. Roberta was back about a hundred meters. How beautiful this place was, especially with the absence of airplane or car noise!

"Come on!" I waved my arm. "Let's walk the whole shore." She waved but said nothing. Her fine black hair went crazy in the jagged wind.

After a leisure hour of walking and stopping for another cigarette, I waited for her. The wind settled down; the quaking birch reflected the sun like glitter. I lay back on the sand and let the sun warm me again. A hawk glided high overhead. As I waited, I heard the familiar bird call of a chickadee. It sounded like a swing rocking slowly forward and back. When I looked up, I saw it fly to the bark of a tree, get its food, and go into the leaves to eat. I cherished this quiet; it was so different from time with my kids, teaching, counseling, and school. Camping and hiking with Roberta were relaxing.

Roberta caught up to me while I was still sitting on the boulders.

"What's wrong?" I sat up.

Her legs were spread for support. She bent over with both hands on her knees and threw up.

"Roberta! What can I do?" When I stood next to her, I could smell the booze. "You've been drinking?" She looked up with spit dangling from her mouth. "But it's still morning." I backed away from her.

She snapped at me. "I'm on fucking vacation! I want no judgment from you!"

Whoa, I thought, *this is a different Roberta from the caring, sweet friend who gave me a rose on a first date.* I felt crazy inside, like when Mom criticized me for no reason or when Ken accused me of having sex with our neighbor across the street.

My gut turned up and down. I said in a quiet but firm voice, "Roberta, don't ever talk to me like that again."

We walked back in silence. I kept an eye on her. She seemed to be stumbling. The trip was ruined.

I calculated my situation; I wondered if Roberta was a viable choice of a companion after all. My warm feelings dissipated, and I began to distance myself.

Chapter 41

I waited in line in my crimson graduation cap, the gold tassel hanging just behind my ear.

"Mary Elizabeth Spray." I stepped up the four shiny wooden steps and crossed the lighted stage, heading for Dr. Bowman, who stood by a table of diplomas.

Mine was the first master's degree in my family.

The full impact of my accomplishment was exhilarating: a master's in second languages and cultures. I looked into the audience and smiled at the support I received from my children and family members who attended the graduation. I thought of the graduation ceremony in Winona I had missed when I received my BA in French right before marrying Ken. It had seemed logical to save money before our wedding. We'd decided I would do my student teaching in Pierre instead of Winona. Before the last semester of my senior year, I left the College of Saint Teresa and student-taught in Pierre. Saint Teresa's was a ten-hour drive away, but the real reason I missed graduation was that Ken and I had not spent much time together before he proposed, and we needed to get acquainted.

Dr. Bowman, my advisor, shook my hand. She was the professor who had been most impressed with my thesis on teaching reading in a second language. To celebrate my achievement, my family, my children, my neighbors, and Karl and Debra were all invited to my graduation party.

Roberta ordered hors d'oeuvres and champagne for the party. We put in all the leaves to expand the table. There was a streamer of "Congratulations!" that hung on the archway between the dining and living room. We arranged the furniture against the walls so our guests could walk and mingle or sit down with a plate on their laps. It was 1990. I was forty, and Gabrielle was fifteen. The boys were twelve and nine. Mom seemed pleased, which was still important to me. She wore a lipsticked "company smile" that I remembered from when I was a child. Mom walked around my table commenting on every little sandwich, the cheese plate, the veggies, and the dip. A cheesecake that said "Congratulations, Mary Beth!" sat in the middle of the table beside yellow roses in a vase.

"How's my sweet granddaughter?" my mom said as she pulled Gabrielle close to her in a tight hug. "You're so grown up, honey." Gabrielle smiled at the compliment and kept her arms around her grandma's waist.

Family and friends started arriving.

"How nice, Mary Beth. You have so many canapes and hors d'oeuvres. Your table looks lovely."

"Well, Mom, Roberta did this for me. She arranged it all." I wanted Mom to like her. I put my hand on Roberta's back and corralled her over to Mom. My family had already met Roberta. She was sober for the party and told me she was not going to drink. She wore a suit jacket and skirt. Her hair was tied in the back with a white scarf. She smiled a lot and looked pretty. Even though I'd come out to my family, no one referred to my relationships as gay or me as a lesbian. It was unspoken, just like the pain and alcohol in our family growing up. My family went out of their way to not talk about Roberta, Melo, or what I did with my relationships. That hurt and felt dismissive. I desperately wanted to talk about Melo and Roberta. Mom always talked with me about Ken. But no one, except Lucy, would talk to me about Melo or Roberta. Maybe it was me who was afraid to bring up my relationships for fear that my family would ignore me further.

"Thanks, Mom, for all the financial help you gave me this last semester." We hugged. Mom had helped me out because I was in such a crisis. My last bill had been for two thousand dollars. She saw that my financial struggles were mainly because Ken did not give regular child support and that I was without a permanent job. Her checks to me were a giant way of showing her love and belief in me. She and my siblings also gave me and my children wonderful birthday and Christmas gifts.

"You're welcome, sweetheart. Your Grandpa's certificates of deposit helped. He would be proud of you." I thought of Grandpa; the smell of his whiskey-whiskered kisses permeated the walk, along with the or-ange-and-yellow columbines in his garden.

Debra and Karl stayed and talked to Ray and Brandon, our neighbors. They drank champagne and laughed. Debra and I always joked that we didn't recognize each other in real clothes outside of jogging attire. Karl loved to tell the story of how Debra and I met in Pierre. Her family had moved to Pierre at the beginning of my senior year in high school. I'd walked the three blocks over to her house, knocked on her door, and asked her if she wanted to be my friend. We'd been friends ever since.

I opened a card from my brother. It said, "Did you ever think this day would come? We didn't either!" Everyone laughed as I read it out loud. My kids hung around for a while but soon slipped into their rooms.

Lucy and her husband stayed a bit longer. She always stood by my choic-es in relationships and whatever I was dealing with. She helped me find jobs and often took me to lunch.

Roberta's friend arrived at 11:00 p.m. After the last of my guests left around midnight, I helped put the hors d'oeuvres away. The plan was that her friend would stay overnight with my kids while Roberta and I went out.

Roberta orchestrated a massive surprise. I was tired from the day's fes-tivities, but took a deep breath, put a smile on my face, and primed myself for the next event. She put a blindfold on me and took me to a Comfort Inn, where she opened the door to a big suite with a whirlpool bath in the middle of the room. She had more champagne chilling in an ice bucket and started the bath right away. I was tired and a bit tipsy from the champagne I'd already consumed. I knew what she was planning. As caring as she tried to be, I was not up for the orgasm trick she showed me using the jets. I lay down on the bed. She poured some champagne into two plastic champagne glasses.

I sat up. "Roberta, sweetheart, I liked the party, but I can't drink any-more. Plus, I'm tired."

She set the glasses down on the end table and sat on the end of the bed. "Yes, Mary Beth, let me hold you until you fall asleep." She brushed my hair behind my ear. "You're a graduated party pooper, aren't you?" she said in a baby voice while patting my hips. "Let's get our jammies on and curl up together."

She did these thoughtful things for me financially. She put on a gradu-ation party, took me out to dinner, and bought me clothes and trips. She tried hard to show her love for me. And the ultimate would have been the house if I would have said, "Let's do it!" I felt obligated to keep on trying to make the relationship work. I was still attracted to someone based on how they would take care of me. Roberta's financial caring was prominent.

As I watched her increasingly drink more, I began to think about why I was here, why I was with her. I tended to fall back into making her happy. Her drinking was distressing me, especially that night, when we were supposed to be celebrating this landmark in my life. I also realized I did more drinking with her than I ever had before.

Male or female, I was still attracted to the broken personality where alcohol lurked somewhere in the background.

Why have I spent my life getting close to sick people? Of all my relationships, my tie to Jesus remained the only unbroken one. I knew he would never leave me.

Every morning when I wrote my prayers and supplications in my notebook, I surrendered to my higher power. The serenity prayer often calmed me: *God grant me the serenity to accept the things I cannot change, the courage to change the things I can, and the wisdom to know the difference.*

I reviewed the alcoholic relationships in my life. I was experiencing the same shit with Roberta. She drank, I got mad, then I felt guilty for not giving her more attention. I always ended up feeling bad.

At breakfast in the motel the next morning, she offered to tell me what had happened at Angela's cabin in Spooner with Melo.

"Mary Beth, I feel I need to get honest with you about that weekend."

"What happened at Angela's cabin?" I finally dared to expel in one breath.

She cleared her throat. "You're sure you want to hear this?" I nodded. "First of all, MB, we got drunk." I looked away, not relishing the rest.

Roberta proceeded to tell me that she and Melo had taken turns going down on Angela. I was satisfied to finally put that behind me because I often wondered what had happened.

Chapter 42

Char and I walked out of the group together. The light-green stairwell's peeling paint revealed yellow patches underneath.

"Teaching sounds cool," she said. We reached the basement. She opened the door for me. I put the straps of my red fake-leather purse over my shoulders.

"Your job sounds cool too! A power line installer? You climb up those poles?" I looked up into her eyes. "It must be dangerous." I felt again my attraction to strong, capable women who did not need help, especially from men.

She shrugged. "Yeah, it pays well. But–"

"But what?" My hand lightly caressed the parking fence.

"The men I work with are obnoxious. They hang pictures of naked women in our workroom where I pack my tools into my grip. I just rip them down." She gestured with her hand in a fist.

"Anyway. Would you teach me Spanish? I'll pay you." We stood outside in the autumn afternoon sun.

"Sure." I beamed. "My car isn't working now—my daughter totaled it."

"I can pick you up at Sanford after school. It's in my neighborhood; then we can go to a restaurant."

"OK, tomorrow after school. Two o'clock?"

During the group session, Sharon, the smoker, offered to give me a ride home. I headed for her beat-up Toyota truck. The back of her truck had all the letters missing except for the "YO." I laughed. We both lit up cigarettes in her car. It was always a relief to have a smoke after the group ended because it was so intense.

"So, it looks like you and Char had things to talk about." She turned to me and winked as she backed out of the parking spot.

"Yeah, I'm liking what I see." I did not want to divulge too many feelings. It felt too soon. But I was bubbling over with tingles. "I'm joining the writers' group that our leader suggested. We meet at one another's homes."

"You write lots already?"

"Yeah, mostly poetry, stuff I'm feeling. And prayers."

"You write out your prayers? How?"

"Well, I start out writing what I'm thankful for. Then whatever comes to mind that I am worried about. Mostly stuff about my kids and their safety."

"Do you think He–does God answer?"

"*She?* Yes, I do. How are you doing with the group, Sharon?" I shifted in my seat, not wanting to make Sharon uncomfortable.

"I can only take so much and then I need a smoke. This shame shit is taking a toll on me."

The next day, seeing Char sitting in her car after school waiting for me, I felt a flutter in my stomach. She looked sexy sitting with one knee up on the dashboard reading.

Eager to please, I stuck cute flirty notes in Spanish on her dashboard, and she eagerly translated them. I prepared them in the math class I subbed for that day. She picked me up the rest of the week. We had one sit-down formal Spanish lesson, and then it petered out. I think she asked me to teach her because that was her way of getting to know me.

Sometimes she took me home, and occasionally we went for walks. I fell fast and hard for her over the next few weeks; the mix of her patchouli and underarm odor became my favorite scent. She introduced authors to me. I wanted to know the books as she did. She was a nice distraction from Melo and Roberta. *Oh, Roberta.* I had to talk to her.

In the next week's ACA group, two members had started dating–the redhead, named Tennessee, and the woman with the long stringy hair. They gazed at each other and held hands. It happened fast. We had a discussion on dating boundaries within the group.

Paula, the leader, said, "Sometimes when we don't learn from our pain, we go from one lousy situation to another. We need time to heal and figure out what's causing our pain."

"I feel guilty when I want to end a hurtful relationship," I said, thinking about Roberta and even Ken.

"You don't need to feel guilty about taking care of yourself, Mary Beth."

I took in a deep breath to think.

Sharon added, "I don't pay attention to my pain."

Paula continued, "We can lessen our suffering by listening to ourselves and what we need."

I mentioned that Char and I were hanging out, and Paula warned me about boundaries.

The group ended with Paula's question, "How do each of you work in your higher power when dealing with your pain? Whoever or whatever he, she, or it is?"

"Mine is my car. It's got me places," Sharon said.

Tennessee said, "My HP is my grandmother." She looked up at the ceiling. "She endured some real shit being married to Grandpa. I just think of her, and I get strength."

"Mine is Jesus," I said. The room went quiet. My heart was beating fast. Char glared at me, then looked away with her chin in hand.

"Well," I started gingerly. "You know, most of the world lives by the date of his birth. Even the nonbelievers." I looked at Char; she rolled her eyes and shook her head like I was an idiot.

Walking down the stairs of the group meeting, she snapped, "What was all that about?"

"Char–"

"Don't ever say shit like that in my presence again."

"You just interrupted me!" I countered, feeling the heat rise.

She stopped with her arms folded.

"Char, my higher power is my business, and I'll talk about Jesus whenever I want." Then I changed the subject. "You found a place? Where?" I looked up at her.

"Near Thirty-Eighth and Bloomington. Mary Beth, I'm going to need time to move and separate from my lover and her daughter." Her fingers combed through her shoulder-length black hair.

Feeling rejected, I looked away and took a big breath. "I'll back away." I leaned on the railing.

"Mary Beth"—she put her face in front of me and grabbed my pony-tail—"not too far. Her small eyes squinted in a smile. "After I get settled, I want to meet your kids."

"Sure!" I relaxed inside. I wanted to learn more about what made her tick. I felt guilty that I was intending to date someone else, because I could still hear the last counselor saying I should wait a year and get to know my-self. I desperately needed someone else in my life to mirror, someone who would help me forget about not liking myself.

When I got home, I called Roberta for a walk around Diamond Lake. I planned to break up.

Chapter 43

As we walked through the dirt path encircling Diamond Lake, I told Roberta that I needed space because of her drinking. I was not being completely truthful; I told her I wouldn't date anyone else.

The next evening toward dusk, a car pulled into the driveway. Char had just dropped me off and was still in her truck. The car's lights shone on us like a spotlight. Char slowly got out of the car, stood up to her full five feet ten inches, and stared. She had one foot on the opened car rim and kept her arms folded. Roberta's friend exited her car and approached me with the lime-green fanny pack that I had given to Roberta.

Char took a step forward.

"Stay here, Char!" I warned.

I walked toward Roberta's friend, hoping to get this over with as soon as possible. Roberta sat in the passenger seat with the ends of her puffy mouth turned down. I went over to her window and motioned for her to crank it down.

"What?" she barked.

"Roberta . . ." I took a big breath. "Our relationship is over because of your drinking." Her head bowed. "Sorry I lied about not dating anyone else." I walked up to her friend.

"Roberta wants the leather butt pack she gave you." She narrowed her eyes. Her hair was short and messy. The shadows on her face from the car lights on her back made her seem ominous. She waited while I went into the house to get it. Char stood guard. They left.

Relieved, I kissed Char good-night on the cheek. "Thanks for sticking around."

I went into an empty house. The kids were at Ken's. I felt bad that I hadn't told Roberta that I'd started up with Char. I heaved a sigh of relief that it was done with her.

When she was not working, Char continued to come by Sanford after 2:00 p.m. She knew some cool places in the city. We walked on a boardwalk over a marsh on the east side of the Mississippi one day; the crickets mixed with the dry matted reeds reminded me that fall was all around us. Cattails poked through the long, slender stalks, some ten feet high. We sat on the edge with our legs crossed. She laid her head on my lap as the sun descended through the tall cottonwoods. Her voice was soft and girly.

"Do you read Louise Erdrich or Barbara Kingsolver?"

"No?"

"I'm reading *Tracks*. What are you reading?"

I laughed. "I don't have time to read. Let's get going. The kids are coming home soon." But I took note of the books she read in hopes of reading them sometime.

Our shoes tapped the boardwalk as we hurried to the car. The next weekend was Halloween.

That weekend, I knocked on the door of Char's new apartment. The Indigo Girls were playing on her CD player. She hesitated before she invited me in.

I was anxious to see her own living space. I hoped there wouldn't be another confrontation with an ex. She had incense and had just made tempeh sandwiches with Indian hot pickle. Seeing a single woman's apartment was exciting for me. Since I had never had one alone, I soaked everything in. So far, most of my furnishings were functional, but someday I hoped that I could add art into my living space. Her place was decorated with the warm earth tones of feng shui. It was cozy and welcoming. A book with pictures of Madonna with other artists in varying stages of undress was displayed on the coffee table. On the wall were the vibrant colors of a Jane Evershed print.

"Do you want some tea?"

"Sure." I glanced around to see what else she had on the walls.

She sipped her hot tea slowly, keeping the cup near her mouth. We sat down and lunched on her sandwiches. I had never tried tempeh before. It was chewy like meat, and the Indian pickle sauce made it spicy.

My surprise visit extended through the whole weekend. There was a huge snowstorm and blizzard-level winds. I worried about my recently bought used car sitting outside in the back. We listened to CDs and cassettes of George Michael and k.d. lang. We ate vegetarian chili and dal—all prepared by Char. I was amazed at how much effort she put into her recipes compared to my easy dishes for the kids. Most of all, I loved having someone cook exotic foods for me. School was canceled on Monday; so was her work. We settled into love-making and sweet conversation. When she talked about issues pertinent to her, I noticed many of them were political. I began to learn how Indigenous people, Black people, women, and gay people were all alienated from power and money. My eyes opened to these issues.

When I finally left our little weekend love nest, the streets and alleys were a mess. Ice ruts made it hard to drive.

After a month passed, I still had not told the kids about my new relationship with Char. She said she would come over on the next snowfall. When it finally snowed, she walked in with a big basket of fruit wrapped in bright cellophane and sat down at the dining room table with her big boots and black jacket. She loosened a black-and-white scarf around her neck. The scarf looked Moroccan, with intricate curvy designs. It was very exotic. She was dressed in black. Her snowcap was the only pop of color. It was red and yellow with tassels hanging down the sides of her face. She sat at the kitchen table with her elbow on her knee.

Gabrielle came up from her basement room in sweats.

"Gabrielle, this is Char," I said.

Char smiled. She slouched in her jacket and hat.

"Hi," Gabrielle said. "Mom, where are my jeans? The stonewashed ones?" Then she noticed the fruit with a smile. That nutritious gift was needed in our house.

"On the dryer."

The boys came down from upstairs. "Chris, Paul, this is Char."

"Where did we get that big basket of fruit?" Gabrielle was already opening the ribbons to get at the oranges.

Char finally spoke up. "I brought the fruit. I don't know–something healthy to have around." She pushed back her ski cap a bit and revealed more dark hair.

The kids were quiet and stared at her.

Then I asked, "Who wants to go tubing?"

Chris looked up and raised his hand. "I do!"

Gabrielle said, "But it's dark out."

"That's the best time to go," Char said with a smile. "There are flood-lights, and you can rent these big tubes."

"Whoever wants to go better hurry up and get dressed, 'cause Char's taking us to slide down the biggest hill in Minneapolis!" They all scrambled.

Chapter 44

When Easter came, Mom said Char was not invited to the family gathering. My family had met Char at Christmas and again at a party at my brother's house. I furiously asserted my gay rights and declared that we all were not coming if Char was not invited. I cried on the phone and so did Mom. My kids and Char sat around the table watching me cry. Char left, and Gabrielle went to Nick's house. The boys and I drove to McDonald's. The consequence of standing up to Mom was six months of silence between us. I felt abandoned by Mom.

Lucy finally put a stop to the cold war between us by insisting I come to her son's birthday party. The kids and I showed up at Lucy's home like nothing ever happened.

Another standoff with Mom had happened ten years earlier, while I was still married and living in Pierre. She was having problems with Dad's drinking and his affair. I'd walked in on her crying alone at the table, which was strewn with placemats and a tablecloth. She talked of not wanting to live anymore. I wanted to pray with her but was not sure how she'd take it. Her shoulders were shaking under her sobs. I sat next to her. The morning light from the east covered her. I gently put my arm around her. I asked her in a soft voice if she wanted me to pray with her and suggested seeing a therapist. Her tear-filled eyes had turned into daggers and bored into me. "What? Are you calling me crazy? Is this Ken's doing?"

Her mother, my grandma, died during that time. With Ken at my side, I called Grandma's home in South Dakota to hear how she was. I volunteered to come and see Grandma. I was close to Grandma and wanted to tell her one last time that I loved her. Mom was there with her siblings and Grandpa. My uncle answered, we conversed about Grandma, and he asked if I wanted to speak with anyone else. I hesitated. Ken looked at me. I said no.

I found out later that Mom burst into tears after I hung up. I regretted not reaching out to Mom. We had not talked for almost two stubborn years back then, and the silence continued even after my third child was born.

A year after Paul was born, I greeted Mom at Frank's wedding. She stood alone in the St. John's Church vestibule.

"Hi Mom, meet your one-year-old grandson." I pushed the stroller up to her. She was the only one in my family who hadn't met Paul. The organist was playing inside the church.

Mom had lost weight. Her hair was in a beauty-shop beehive style. She was divorced and had just arrived from her home in St. Paul. She looked stressed. Dad was somewhere in the church also.

"Hi, Mary Beth." Her voice was one low, even pitch.

She did not make a move to embrace me or Paul. I longed for her to reach out and touch me. I took my toddler out of the stroller and brought him face to face with Mom. His smile opened to her along with his curly head of hair. She finally smiled.

She loved my babies.

When Gabrielle was born, six years before Paul, Mom had come straight to the hospital and waited. I had called her the night before to let her know I was in labor. I remember my bed being pushed out of the post-delivery room into the bright light of the reception area. I had my baby in my arms. I could hear buzzers going off and women talking. My newborn still had cheesy stuff on her sweet head. When I looked up, tears had welled in Mom's eyes as she looked down on us.

"Look at my baby girl, Mom."

"She's beautiful, Mary Beth." Her voice sounded loving. Mom took a strand of my sweaty hair and moved it away from my face. "She has rosebud lips." She seemed emotional; she was trembling. "When I heard you were in labor, I came straight here. I've been sitting here for quite a while. I know how grueling labor can be."

I felt our connection as mothers, something only a mother and daughter can share. I will never forget her expression of love for me that day.

Later, I found out from her that Ken had not allowed her to come into the post-delivery room.

I didn't want to lose my connection with Gabrielle. Her weight gain and puffy face, I eventually found out, were signs of the eating disorder bulimia. I felt like a bad mom. The toilet-flushing surfaced in my memory—especially when she was upset.

Big portions of cake were gone, but my life was so busy that I was glad when the food was eaten. I never investigated. And when she volunteered to bake a cake, I was pleased that she wanted to help. She worked at the Chinese takeout, and then she chose a French takeout. She brought food home.

Gabrielle stumbled into the house early one evening. She held on to the table in the entryway. I approached her and saw her blurry eyes. She surrendered into my arms, smelling of alcohol. I took her downstairs, gave her a pan to throw up in, and put her to bed.

She was safe in her bed, but what happened next caught me off guard.

It was early spring, and dusk extended into the night. Char and I had just come home from dinner. She left her truck in front of the garage, and we walked the long driveway toward the front yard. We heard angry voices arguing, which drowned out the 35W highway noise. It was my sixteen-year-old Gabrielle, her friend Rachel, and some other kids I didn't know. Gabrielle ran to us from the front yard when she noticed we had arrived.

"Mom, the police were just here!" Her back-combed hair and side flips drooped, and her face looked blotchy. Kids were yelling at each other in the front yard.

"Why? What happened?"

"Nick hit me, and Rachel called the police. When the police questioned if Nick hit me, I said no." Gabrielle avoided my alarmed eyes. Then she faced me with a red imprint of a hand on her cheek.

"Mom! I was scared; I didn't know what to do. He gave me a real hard, mean stare when the cops were asking me questions. Rachel's mad at me. That's not all, Mom. Look at the side door." Her eyes looked to the other side of the house. It was dark, and I went around to the north side of the bungalow house that Melo and I had rented together just two years before. On the side door, a glass window had been smashed in. There was glass everywhere inside and out, along with blood.

Char stood speechless and observed the next few minutes as a bystander, her arms crossed and eyes squinting.

"Karl came to get Nick. He needs stitches. I'm sorry, Mom!" She came to my arms and settled in, head on my chest. We sat down together on the kitchen stools. It was cold in the kitchen because of the broken window. I had a thousand questions.

"What's this about, Gabrielle?"

Her rosebud lips quivered.

"I wanted to break up with Nick but didn't tell him till tonight when Donny came over. He and I were going downstairs. Then Nick showed up."

Exhausted and depleted, I put my hair up in a ponytail. "Help me find something to cover the window. Char? Can you help me out here?" I called out her name. "Where is she?"

"I'm in the living room," she yelled from around the corner.

"I need your help, Char; how do you think I should cover this window?" She walked into the kitchen and did an about-face.

"Char?"

In the middle of all this chaos and trauma, Char stomped her foot and said, "I'm leaving. Going home! I don't do this kind of male violence on women!"

Alone, deserted, and afraid, I called Debra. I realized that I hadn't thought of how Karl and Debra, or even Nick, might feel. Karl answered when I called Debra's number. He started crying.

"Karl, how is Nick?"

"I just brought him back from the hospital. He had stitches."

"Karl, I have a broken window here. Can you come over and fix it? It's midnight and I'm scared."

He addressed me in the firmest voice I had ever heard from him. "Mary Beth, I just got back from the hospital. My son has tendons severed. I can't."

He stopped sobbing after a minute on the phone. Karl was one of the sweetest men I knew. All women my age adored him. He was attentive when talked to. He always offered to help. But this time, I let him be.

Exhausted and cold, I found a handsaw and some nails that were too large in the shadowy garage and sawed a piece of particle board from a drawer to fit the broken window. I pounded the board onto the door.

Gabrielle and I went to the city hall the next day.

Together, we filled out the forms and paid the ninety dollars to put a restraining order on Nick, my best friend's son. I didn't have the wherewithal to file charges against Nick for assaulting Gabrielle. The best I could do was to file a restraining order.

Three weeks later, we went to court. Debra and her family were on one side, and Gabrielle and I were on the other. The courtroom seemed dark. Debra's brother, an attorney, represented Nick. He pleaded "no contest." He didn't look at us for a long while, and then he came over with his bandaged hand upright.

"Mary Beth, Gabrielle, I want to apologize to you for the pain I caused."

"Thank you for saying that, Nick." He seemed docile and pale.

Gabrielle said nothing and looked straight ahead. We didn't greet Debra and Karl.

This took a toll on my relationship with Debra. It was a while before either of us would mend. A few weeks later, the next time we met to go running, Debra and I cried together on the 35W bridge. It was windy, and the traffic noise was deafening.

"Them getting together was not a good idea," I said, wiping my eyes.

"No, it was not, and Karl was right. They never should have dated."

Several years before, Karl had expressed concern about Nick and Gabrielle dating. Nick was two years older, and Karl had felt Gabrielle was too young.

"We blew it, Debra, encouraging them as we did." She nodded and wiped her eyes.

I told her that I should have questioned their relationship when I found out they were drinking. But Gabrielle is stubborn like me. I once refused to listen to my mother when she was concerned about Ken.

"Are you OK, Mary Beth?"

"Yes." We hugged for a long time. Then we ran down to the creek. "Will you give Karl a big hug from me?"

"Do it yourself!"

I smiled. Debra was back to her old self.

I dropped by Char's house to tell her how angry I felt with her about her bolting the scene. I understood that the violence was disconcerting to Char. But I needed an adult to help me care for my daughter and to make my home feel safe that evening. *Maybe I don't need anybody anymore. I did take care of the mess on my own.* I'd thought Char would be this lovely addition to my life, and all I got was a narcissistic woman. She once stormed out of a movie theater and slammed the theater door over a wimpy female role in the film. I was shocked. When I came out at the end of the movie, she was talking to her ex on a pay phone. She had jealous bouts over women giving me attention. She had some layers of anger that I was not sure I wanted to peel.

I stood at the door. "Why did you leave when I needed you the most, Char?" Looking for a comparison I said. "If something happened to your cats, I would help you and not leave."

Morrissey music was playing inside her house. Her life seemed so peaceful.

I took in a breath. "I know you also had a violent dad, and this might be an issue for you, but I needed a partner and not a deserter." I had felt abandoned.

She leaned against the door. "I can't be around that kind of male aggression. You have not trained your daughter enough on how to run from a violent man. Maybe she learned from you." Her deadpan face just stared back at me.

Chapter 45

Once I discovered Gabrielle's bulimia, I wanted to support her, so I searched for a therapist.

"Um, sweetheart, where did you learn about throwing up?" I put my elbows on my knees.

"Actually, Mom, it was at Christian summer camp. All the Edina girls lined up after lunch and supper, went into the stalls, and forced a finger down their throats. I heard them."

She'd been fourteen and fifteen those summers.

It was a relief for me to have a therapist, another adult, to help care for her. I knew she needed help, and I knew that I didn't know how to guide her through an eating disorder. I welcomed a knowledgeable therapist. At sixteen, she looked sad and red-cheeked with puffy bangs and lots of hair spray. Clothes were an issue for her, as they were for most teenagers. My clothes were smaller than hers. She borrowed clothes from friends. We could not afford much, and most of her outfits were ill fitting.

Every time I picked her up, I was dying to find out how the counseling sessions went. In the first meeting with her counselor, we agreed to privacy for Gabrielle. Her therapist was warm and inviting but down to business. She was about my age and dressed in a suit jacket and pants.

After a few sessions, Gabrielle started getting a bit more talkative; she understood more. She seemed relaxed as she jumped into the Toyota and shared how the counselor did not judge. Gabrielle said that she liked her.

"How's the time with your counselor today, Gabrielle?" I said with a smile and mustered enthusiasm. I lit a cigarette. I was tired from chauffeuring the kids. I'd picked her up right after I dropped Chris at his drum lesson, and Paul was waiting for me at Ricky and Larry's house.

"Mom, I have something to tell you."

"Oh, great, tell me," We did not talk much back then.

"I'm not a virgin anymore."

Silence.

I screamed and turned toward her, my hands on the wheel. "You're what?" She leaned back against the headrest and closed her eyes.

"*You whore!*" I blurted.

We both started crying. I steered, looking across at her, ready to burst. I pulled over. *What did I just say? How could I not have empathy for her? Why was I so quick to be judgmental?* I felt ashamed and that I was a bad mom.

"Mom, it started with Nick, and now with Donny." I lit another cigarette and filled the car with smoke. She rolled down the window and coughed.

As soon as I got home, I called her boyfriend's parents. This was un-fortunately the first time I had talked to them. They seemed calm and said little. Gabrielle seemed relieved, like a weight had been lifted. I also talked to Debra and Karl about our children having sex.

The word *whore*—where had it come from? I don't remember my family ever using it with me or anyone else. Movies, naughty boys in the neigh-borhood? I know I'd felt like a whore during Ken's accusations; I had felt judged, shamed, bad, and embarrassed. And that was the word I called my daughter. My beautiful, loving daughter was right in a decisive moment of vulnerability, and I blew it. I was so consumed with my pain that I was blind to what she was going through. Hurt can be selfish. Misery can make you ignore the vulnerable.

I called Kate, a friend from my writing group. She walked me through the twelve-step program, listened, and told me I was a good mother. I prayerfully went back to those words God gives me when I listen. *Mary Beth, you are precious to me—I love you, and nothing you do will change that.*

It took me a month to wallow in my shame. Then I asked her, "Honey, will you forgive me for calling you that name?"

"Mom, don't worry about it."

I apologized to Gabrielle several more times until I forgave myself. A weight lifted.

Chapter 46

"Usually, I don't go to men's sports." Char looked down at me, her mouth tight and tiny. "Especially baseball. You know, a bat and a ball. It's so about men's genitals."

Her comment made me think, and it was true in a sense, but I tried to ignore her because I was wondering why I was still with her. I had big problems with letting go of relationships.

"We're sitting here; these are little boys, Char. And my son." I laid the blanket down behind the home-plate fence, ignoring her. She had made comments about Chris and how he treated his girlfriends. I don't think she had been around teenagers very much. I cleared my throat several times. I sat up tall to see if Ken was standing around. Char positioned herself with one knee up and an elbow resting on it.

"Oh no!" she said sideways under her breath. "Look who's coming!" Appearing from the adjoining ball field was Melo. She marched in front of the viewers along the baseline. Her hair floated with each step.

"Don't talk to her, Mary Beth! I am warning you! I can't handle an ex of yours of any kind!" Char said out of the side of her mouth.

I shifted away from Melo when I saw her approach. Deep down, I was happy to see her. In almost two years, I had only seen her two times: when she brought over the dancer ceramic gift, and up north at a Minnesota women's music festival the previous spring. I'd pointed Melo out to Char then.

Melo had been selling her painted rocks in a booth. She saw me from afar. Many of her painted rocks had four figures, an adult female and three children. I'd held one in which a woman and the three kids had been painted artfully in her style. Melo had offered it to me.

Out of the corner of my eye, I could still see Melo quietly standing and smiling as Char led me to another area of the small festival.

The boys' teams huddled. Melo stood by my blanket, her sneakers together.

"Hi, Mare!" With a big grin, her hand up by her head, she gave a quick side-to-side wave. "Hi, Char." Char glared, and I said nothing. I retied my sneakers to keep from looking at her. Hesitantly, Melo sat next to me. I pretended to watch the game, but no one was playing at that moment. I leaned back on both hands, so I could see more of her on the periphery. Her hair was even longer, and her clothes were different, looser, like when I'd seen her up north selling her rock art. She leaned forward, turned in front of me, and tried again.

I wanted to ask what had brought her there. Was there a child she was watching? But I did not dare with Char breathing down my back. My deep feelings for Melo hadn't fully disappeared. I'd never go back into a relationship with her, but I still cared for her.

"It must be halftime," I said with a half smile and a side glance.

Melo gave a big laugh at my nonchalant/on-purpose mix-up of sports terms, just as she had always done with Chris. She took a deep breath and ended it with a hum. I knew that breath and hum meant she was happy. Char, who was silent, gave me a nudge with her foot. I kept looking at the empty ball field. I had questions I wanted to ask Melo.

Melo looked back to where she'd come from and started fidgeting. Glancing sideways, I saw that her eyes were filling with tears. I wanted to hug her. The next thing I knew, Melo's back was disappearing down the line from where she had come. This time, her hair bounced with the stomp and her shoulders bent forward.

Ignoring her made me feel sick inside. I wanted to run after her and apologize but stayed immobile. I had questions about how she was doing and who the larger woman was who was with her. I avoided Char's crimpled face. When someone was uncomfortable with my behavior, I couldn't express my deep-down desires. Yet my obedience began to bug me. When we got in the car, we argued about Melo again. I felt shame for wanting to talk with Melo and not pleasing Char. I had visions of Melo sitting next to me, wondering where the muzzle was that kept me from talking or looking at her. I felt nauseous and yanked my hand away from Char's when she grabbed it.

It was just like when Ken had forbade me to talk to Leeanne. He'd questioned why we studied koine Greek together to see what the Bible said or did not say about the feminine. Ken's control over me had been solid. I did whatever he wanted back then.

Char knew my love for Melo was still there deep down. I brought up Melo from time to time. She knew I'd left a man for Melo. I told Char that Melo and I had a deep connection. Char flitted from one relationship to another and was afraid I would do the same. We went to therapy for a while to deal with her impatience with my boys and even her attraction to other women. She said she was attracted to the nurturing mother and teacher in me.

So far, I had chosen insecure partners who found a hook, a hold on my naivete. Or maybe it was the opposite. Maybe I looked for strong women who had qualities I lacked. I knew I had qualities to offer a life partner. But I had thirty-five years of practice doing what an authority figure said and leaning on a male's opinion. That was gradually unraveling. Pleasing others still dragged me back to my old ways and was my armor. When I took it off, I felt vulnerable. Then, eventually, strong.

I prayed. *God, I need an intervention. Give me the courage to end this relationship or send my lover into an orbit around me, more focused on me. Let her be less clingy and selfish with money. Let her care for me, do sweet things for me, scratch my back.* When I prayed, I let go of that problem I prayed about. But I still struggled with ending a hurtful relationship.

I learned a lot about myself dating Char. She gradually opened my eyes to liberal politics, social equality and inequality, female authors, vegetarian cooking, and being a self-reliant lesbian. I will forever be grateful to her for that. But she was also controlling and told me what to eat, which movies not to watch, which friends not to have, and how to accommodate her and her lifestyle. And I had followed.

Chapter 47

My last argument with Char centered around her anger with the movie *Sleepless in Seattle*. Sitting side by side on a low beige sectional with long pillows that I'd bought at a garage sale, our feet on the beige ottoman and popcorn in a bowl on our laps, we started the movie. The kids were around, passing in and out.

She freaked out. "Why do you like this movie? It's about a boy who finds a woman online." She blinked, her chest heaving.

I did not understand what bothered her. Maybe it was because it was about a straight couple. It was easy to feel invisible in the straight world. But that day I had no tolerance for her angst.

"It's just a movie to enjoy, not destroy." I tried to stay calm. I heard Chris and his friends come in. "Hi, sweetheart." I unlocked from Char's hovering and put on a bright smile for Chris. "There's hot tuna sandwiches on top of the stove." They took one look at her, turned, and each grabbed a sandwich on the way out the back door.

"This movie is not enjoyable to me and—" She started crying. "Why is it enjoyable to you?" I felt sorry for her, but I was not going to be manipulated.

"Ah, hmm, Char. I don't know. It's a touching human story?" My voice lifted in a questioning tone as I put my popcorn bowl on the ottoman and stood up.

"It's about a stupid fucking man's life. What about me?" she whimpered.

I put my finger to my mouth to try and quiet her. She did not get it. Earlier counseling had not helped much. Arguing around the kids was the last straw.

"What about you, Char? What's going on?" I asked, not knowing how to console her.

She got up with a stomp of her feet and put on her black-and-white scarf and jacket. I caught a glimpse of a dribble on her sharp nose as her twisted face turned away from me. All I could see was her dark jacket covering her neck scarf. The pounding of her tall black Doc Martens echoed heavily through the dining room and living room to the front lead-glass door.

Gabrielle glanced in from the kitchen to see the commotion. Her forehead wrinkled in a question. Char stared at Gabrielle and turned loudly, slamming the door. She continued to step noisily across the front porch and down the sidewalk. She banged the door of her SUV and left.

Sheepishly, I looked at Gabrielle; she sighed and disappeared.

I sat down, my own tears welling. *Another failure.* I wondered what was wrong with me. My anger intensified because I had missed the end of the movie. I was embarrassed in front of my daughter, but I did not have the words to explain or comfort Gabrielle. I almost wanted her to comfort me.

Whoa! Things are getting twisted, MB, I said to myself.

The phone rang; it was Char crying. "Are you still watching that movie?"

"No!" I defended myself loudly. "It's long over now. I didn't see the end thanks to you." Silence.

"I don't know, Mary Beth; I'm having a hard time with your hetero world."

"Geez, Char, can you lighten up? It's just a movie!" I felt that familiar shame of not measuring up to someone's qualifications.

"Mom, are you OK?" Gabrielle asked as she approached me.

"Char, I gotta go, bye." The phone rang. I ignored it. It rang and rang, then stopped. A few minutes later, the phone started ringing again. I was uncomfortable at the scene we were making in front of my children. I went to the phone.

"Mom?" Gabrielle gently warned.

I picked up the phone and started biting my nails. Char started ranting without me saying a word. Crying, she sobbed, "Can I come back over?"

"No, Char, you can't. Not tonight."

"But–"

"Char, no!" I hung up.

I found the one cigarette I'd hidden behind the curtains. I went out back for a long pensive smoke. It was dark by then, and the autumn night air was cooling down fast. A few stars were starting to appear under the city lights. Venus was prominent in the southeast.

"Mom, Char's here again," Gabrielle said in a quiet voice through the screen of the back door. The outline of her shadow slowly disappeared.

I got up, readying myself for battle. I took a deep breath; Char's contorted face was still in the door window. She seemed taller and larger; she had her overnight bag on her hip. Her jacket covered her bag and body, so she seemed much larger. Or was it that I felt smaller, like an ant to be stepped on? I didn't want to open the door, but I had never shut the door on anyone. I had never kicked anyone out of my house. I unlocked the deadbolt, and she forced the door open immediately.

"You can't stay!" I said first. She kept crying.

"But baby, why not?" She reached for me, and her eyes darted.

"Char, goodbye. Don't come back."

Chapter 48

I settled back into the rhythm of single parenting. I dropped Chris and his friend Jimmy off at the mall and relaxed for a quiet evening. According to Chris, Jimmy's mom was picking them up.

Jimmy and Chris had met some St. Paul girls at the mall who invited them to a party that weekend. On weekend nights with the kids, I usually crashed at about ten or eleven in the evening. Each one had to wake me up when they came home and breathe in my face, so I could check for alcohol and drugs.

The buzz of the doorbell woke me up. It was close to midnight. I put my robe on and looked out my bedroom window. I saw a squad car.

A tall police officer stood with Chris and Jimmy at the front door. Looking like a polar bear, I tightened my raggedy faux-fur robe with ripped seams and singed cuffs and unlocked the door.

The cop pushed his cap back on his white hair. "Ma'am, is this your son?" he asked. His looming figure, a gun and a baton strapped to his waist, took me aback. Chris stood there, unsmiling, his mouth slightly ajar, his chipped front tooth from a skateboard fall visible. The top of his head was wrapped in a red-bandana neck scarf, a current fad of skateboarders'. Jimmy, also unsmiling, stared at my dark wood floor.

"Yes," I said, my voice shaking.

"He only got around the corner–making so much noise, three times stopping and lurching your car with the clutch. Then it stalled and killed. Well, as the story goes, according to your son here"—he looked down at him—"he was on his way to St. Paul with Jimmy here. I asked your son whose car it was. He said yours. Then I asked if he wanted to go downtown or back home. He said downtown." He shifted to his other leg with a smile. "So I brought him home."

Yeah, I know, I thought. The punishment I would dole out would be severe. I drove stick-shift cars for two reasons: it was cheaper on gas, and it was harder for a child to manage. The cop handed me my car keys.

After his two-week sentence was served, I kept a close eye on Chris's comings and goings. One day I noticed he had a pager. It had suddenly appeared on his slouched waistband.

"Why do you need a pager, Chris?"

"No big deal, Mom, just to keep in touch with my friends."

"But doesn't the phone work?"

"Yeah, but everyone's doing it, and it's fun to see a number, then go to the phone," he said casually.

Later, I vacuumed all the upstairs rooms, setting chairs in the hallway and clearing out stuff under the beds. When I moved Chris's dresser to vacuum, I noticed a lump under the corner of the sculpted gray carpet. It sunk under the pressure of my foot. I got down on my knees, ripped up the carpet, and found a big wad of twenty-dollar bills rolled up with a rubber band. I had never seen that much cash in my hand before–over a thousand dollars. I flipped through it in a hurry because Chris would be home soon from school. *Why am I nervous?* I thought. *This is my house.* I pulled open the sliding doors to the closet, and it did not take long for me to find a big plastic Ziploc bag of marijuana. I had never seen pot up close. It had little buds matted together and loose flakes like dried basil. It did not at all resemble my cigarette tobacco. The window was slightly ajar too.

I met Debra at the park. We started our usual route.

"I found money and grass in Chris's bedroom."

She stopped midstride and looked at me. "Ooooh! That sucks."

"Yeah, I'm thinking of some kind of punishment that actually will probably hurt me more."

The run was good for me. It calmed me down. I had figured out that I needed to vocalize my thoughts, and Debra had always been there to listen.

Chris lounged on my oversized armchair with his eyes closed, listening to Frank Zappa, when I walked in from the run. His stocking cap was pulled down over his eyes, so I could barely see his face.

"Hi, Mom." He pulled up his cap.

"Chris. What do you need a pager for? I thought they were just for doctors and people who needed to be contacted right away."

"Friends, Mom." His eyes darted back and forth.

I went to the cupboard and held up the bag of weed and the roll of twenties. "Is this why you need it?"

He licked his lips. "I forgot I had that money, Mom."

"Under the carpet? This was under a nailed-down carpet!" I was shaking with anger and disbelief.

"Chris!" I swung the bagful of weed in the air. "Dealing is dangerous!" I yelled, feeling like I was losing control.

After flushing the contents of the bag down the toilet, I hoped he would hear all three flushes.

He sat silently, shaking his head.

"We will talk about this tomorrow! In the meantime, you stay home tonight." I wasn't sure how he'd respond. Things seemed out of my control, and I needed to process his behavior.

I was confused. It looked like he was dealing. I knew he'd been kicked out of Washburn High School. Was he dealing now at Southwest High School? Did I have a drug dealer in the house? I ran my fingers through my hair. I thought about it overnight, then called Debra and ran my idea by her. She thought my idea was risky. I hoped it wasn't too harsh. I wanted to make clear to him how serious this was. Then, we could look at treatment. I had to let him know he could go to jail.

Ken would just blame me, so I decided I would tell him later. I wondered how much of this was normal teenage behavior. Chris's smoking pot was, but dealing was not. I had to show some tough love. I prayed on my knees that night. *Dear Jesus, give me wisdom on how to deal with my son whom I love with all my heart.*

"Chris, you're going to have to give me your pager," I told him the following morning.

He laughed. "No way, Mom. I have all my friends' phone numbers in there. Why?" He shifted from side to side.

"Because of the pot and money I found in your bedroom yesterday." My hands opened wide. "Do you know that if you deal within three hundred feet of a school, you can go to prison?"

"Mom, Mom, it's no big deal. Just settle down." His condescending voice further angered me. "The weed is gone now anyway." His eyes looked up to his bedroom.

"I'm afraid, Chris, that I'm going to have to be drastic here. You're a minor, and you can't make these decisions on your own." I looked him in the eyes. "Chris. If you don't hand over the pager by five o'clock this evening, then all your belongings, all your clothes, cassettes, everything will be on the boulevard at five thirty."

"Mom, what are you doing? You're ruining my life!" He spun around with his hands on his head.

"Five o'clock, today." I turned and walked upstairs, very unsure of my decision and the outcome.

Chapter 49

I did not want Chris to be homeless. Standing at the front window, I scanned the quiet street. In front of the house, a few cars slowly motored by, their occupants unaware that my home life could be torn up in the next few hours. Chris left early for school. I worried about the damage the marijuana may have done to his young brain. My research said that it affects memory, especially in adolescents, not to mention the deep burn to his lungs. He had previously dismissed my opinion when I talked about the evils of marijuana. I suspected he had been using the previous year and probably earlier; I just didn't know. He had research that said it was harmless. But it was illegal. I did not want him to turn out like the pothead I met in college who just smiled instead of taking part in conversations. Yes, I only knew one pothead.

I had to call Ken. I wondered if he had any ideas on how to deal with Chris. The remote landline phone stood at attention in its base. After picking it up and taking a deep breath, I told Ken that I had found marijuana.

"What? What is going on over there? Do you have things under control, Mary Beth?"

"Yes, I do, Ken. I'm giving him till five o'clock this evening to give me his pager."

"What the hell is that supposed to do?"

"It's my first step . . ."

"I'm going to have to intervene here and make some phone calls."

My face heated. "You are very welcome to do so, Ken. I would appreciate that. In the meantime, I'll continue to find ways to care for and help Chris."

And I hung up.

I stood guard watching for Chris the rest of the day. My stomach growled, but I could not eat. Would I have to find boxes and start packing his things? I couldn't kick him out; I loved him. He was still my responsibility. I hadn't thought this through. Was I unreasonable? I picked up my prayer notebook and started writing.

Dear Jesus. Keep Chris safe today. Give him wisdom. Put a shield around him–your angels. Give me the courage to follow through on my ultimatum. Bring my baby back to me and clear the shitty smoke out of our lives.

At 4:45 p.m., Chris marched through the front door, left it ajar, and pounded the dark, worn hardwood floor with his Vans. His jacket hung loosely like all his clothes. His eyes bored into me as he halted in front of where I sat at the dining room table. I closed my prayer notebook and waited.

His mouth open, he pulled out his pager from his deep jeans pockets. It was in pieces.

"Here's my pager, Mom. I crushed it with my foot!" he shouted. I could barely see his eyes behind his hair.

He heaved it onto the living room floor. "I'll just get a new one tomorrow!" he yelled, before he stomped out the front door.

I fought back tears and released a deep breath. It felt like I had been holding it in all day. The broken pager lay in plastic shards, shattered all over the floor. Some pieces were spread under the wingback chair and in front of me. I picked up the inside mechanism and turned it around in my hand. It buzzed in my hand and scared me. I put it in a drawer of the oak built-in buffet. I wondered who had contacted him. Were these strangers or his friends who called him? Did Jimmy smoke weed with him? I had no clue who smoked with him or where he sold. I had not been vigilant in checking in with my children. I'd been working, and I'd neglected my other full-time job—the kids. I made myself a cup of chamomile tea and watched the steam rise in front of the late afternoon sun. I had to gather my thoughts and wrapped myself under a green, white, and maroon afghan Susan had crocheted.

I thanked God that there was not a pile of Chris's belongings on the front boulevard grass. I wondered if I really would have moved his stuff to the front yard. Could I have carried out that threat? I was exhausted. It felt like when Ken and I argued. It was as energy draining. But now, I made my decisions by myself. I won that battle with a small victory. I prayed, *Lord Jesus, help me get through just today.*

Chapter 50

If Chris was dealing and using at fifteen, what was Paul doing? He was only twelve. A girlfriend braided his blond curls into tiny braids that stuck straight up. His spirit was sweet. Lately, in middle school, his guitar playing had drawn the attention of the girls in his class. After a short conversation, he told me he'd smoked some of my cigarettes and had tried weed. I had to put a stop to this drug use. I wanted to scare them both.

When I called the Fifth Precinct, I made sure my voice was loud enough that they could hear my request for a drug-sniffing dog to come through the house. The only thing the dog found was a bag of my dried tarragon.

Searching for a drug counselor felt like a guessing game. Ken wanted a Christian counselor. I wanted an official chemical dependency therapist, and that's where we started. After dropping Chris off the first day, I wondered if he would follow through with the counselor. For a month, I took him twice a week to her office in a half basement on Franklin Avenue. She wanted me to just drop him off.

One day, I caught a glimpse of her when I picked Chris up. I hoped the session had been successful.

"How was it today?" I asked before Chris could even shut the car door.

"Good, Mom." His smile encouraged me. I relied on the professional help of his counselor the same way I relied on Gabrielle's counselor. His hair was away from his face, and his eye contact took a load off my heart. I could tell that maybe it was working. She must have won his trust right away. Or maybe he'd realized the possible consequences of dealing and reconsidered. Or worse, maybe something terrible was about to happen and he needed an immediate about-face. I noticed that he did not hang out with certain friends anymore. His serene countenance reminded me of when my dad came out of treatment after telling the truth. They both looked at me with clear eyes.

"You like her?" I wanted to know more, anything. He no longer carried that musty odor around his face and clothes.

"She's cool." He quietly leaned back in the seat and stared out the window.

My heart sang with relief. Again, a counselor helped me parent; I was not tackling this alone. And of course, I had been praying that my son's life would straighten out. But I still did not know if he was using or selling.

The counselor recommended treatment after a month, and that came with a family-week session where the patient's family would show up to support them. I was surprised; I'd thought that just a few counseling sessions would be enough. I obediently arranged the week with the treatment center she recommended. It made me nervous thinking about getting together in the same room with Ken. He and I had several conversations about the severity of Chris's addiction.

He stayed in the center for a week; I visited him several times. It looked like a hospital—he wore a gown for the first few days. The place was well lit. Some kids were playing ping pong. Some were dressed in regular clothes. An aide brought him out.

"Hi, honey. I miss you at home."

"You do?" he joked. "I thought I was a pain in the butt for you."

I frowned. "I never said that, Chris." I had tremendous guilt that my lifestyle as a single mom, not to mention being a lesbian and the yelling and screaming during the years before the divorce, had contributed to his being involved with drugs.

His smile faded too. "Just teasing, Mom. I'm learning here that because you love me you sent me to a therapist, and eventually admitted me to this place." His clear, beautiful eyes stayed with me and gave me peace.

"How long do you wear the gown?"

"This is my last day. I finally stopped the 'stinkin' thinkin',' so I can get dressed tomorrow."

I liked hearing the program vernacular.

"What were you doing before I came?"

He held up a book, *The Te of Piglet*. "I was reading this."

"Can I see?" He handed it to me, and I flipped through it.

"It's about Taoist philosophy."

"I've never read it."

A young man came over. "Excuse me, Chris. It's time for our group."

"Gotta go, Mom."

My spirits lifted after a few more visits and daily phone calls.

On our jog, I let Debra know of Chris's progress.

"You're doing all the right things, Mary Beth. Chris's lucky to have you."

I stopped and held her arm. "Thank you for saying that, Debra. Sometimes I don't know what I'm doing."

Chapter 51

At the end of the week, I showed up along with Ken, his wife Sandra, and other parents for the two-day session. It was a big room–folding chairs with orange seat cushions were arranged in a circle. Windows lined the east wall. Other families were talking and trailing in. I sat opposite Ken and Sandra. Ken wore khakis. His short legs were crossed, and his arms were folded apart from one hand that settled under his chin. He wore a turtleneck under a plaid wool jacket with patches on the elbows. Sandra, his wife, sat up straight in a matching blue jacket and an A-line skirt with a white blouse and red scarf tied at the neck. Their eyes followed me as I came in. I nodded to them. He responded with a nod, and she with a smile.

Chris sat laughing with his treatment buddies, their heads together. He wore his slouchy jeans, Vans, and a Washburn hoodie. He was less sullen and secretive. I got his attention and motioned for him to come to me. He sat in the empty chair next to me.

"Hi, Mom." He wore a big smile.

"How are you doing with all this, sweetheart? Are you nervous?"

He thought quietly for a moment. "I can't say I'm looking forward to this, Mom." He glanced around the room. "But I'll be glad when it's over."

"How was the week?" I wanted him to sit by me for a few more moments. Hoping to put my arms around him, I scooted next to his body.

"The week was hard. I'm working things out about dealing. It's not easy to break out of."

He searched my eyes. "I have"—he paused—"customers." I had not heard him be so honest before. It was refreshing and scary. It reminded me that I had been dishonest with him about loving Melo until I came out as gay. Oh, how I wished I had spoken the truth with my children and hadn't modeled for them how to cover up their true feelings. I almost didn't want to know about his business dealings.

"Are you doing the steps?"

He nodded. "I'm getting back to my friends." He walked back, but before he sat down, he stopped by Ken and Sandra. He embraced them both and then sat with his friends.

Ken rubbed his chin. Sandra just sat there with her hands on her purse in her lap. Ken turned to his wife, leaned in like an attorney does with a client, and said something to her. She nodded as he talked in her ear. Other patients in the treatment center sat between their parents or with a sole parent.

Chris's counselor walked into the room. She had wavy, brown shoulder-length hair. She was a bit overweight and wore jeans and a collared blouse. She sat down in an empty chair in the circle. She smiled at Chris and his new friends from treatment. Then she got up and went over to the kids to say something. They all looked at her when she spoke. She sat back down to begin the meeting with us.

"Welcome, parents and families. We are going to start with each patient here telling us just a few sentences about what they have learned so far."

Chris said similar things to the other kids. "I'm trying to get through just this day without using. My higher power helps." His elbows were on his knees and his eyes were lowered. Then he looked around the room. "I still have a lot of work to do to make amends and get straight." He ended with a glance at me.

When Ken took a turn, I feared that he would set me up as the bad parent like he used to do, but I had confidence that the counselor would make sure there was no blame. When he started speaking, he mentioned that he had authored a book on recovery for kids. Gabrielle had the book at home on her shelf. On the back, I noticed his bio said that he was the proud father of five kids. None of Ken or Sandra's children lived with them. I'd scoffed to myself, knowing it should have said he did not pay regular child support for three of those children of his who gave him pride. Ken continued speaking: "My son stays with his mother, and things have deteriorated over the years." He coughed into his fist. "Something has to change"—he pointed his finger up in the air—"and change fast."

I was exasperated with Ken but kept silent. Then I made an offer: "Ken, you and Sandra are very welcome to have Chris stay at your home." Tired of listening to him, I called his bluff. If it came to a change, Chris would have to agree, so I knew it wouldn't happen.

Chris's eyes bugged out, "Mom!"

"And then I can take the visiting parent role."

Ken came out with, "Wow! Yes, Mary Beth. Finally." He uncrossed his legs and leaned forward.

I stared at him with my arms folded. I was tired of Chris's shenanigans—his drug use and his harassment of Paul—and I'd had enough of Ken's bullshit. I knew he would not take Chris for an extended amount of time; I just wanted to let both know that I would no longer would be easy to manipulate. Ken loved Chris, but he was not prepared to have him 24-7. It was decided at the time of the divorce that Ken would take the kids during the summer. That had never happened.

Ken looked at his wife. "I think we can do this, Sandra. What do you think?"

"What? Are you kidding?" She raised her voice. "We don't have time or space for kids."

"Sandra! This is my son!" Their conversation blew up into a screaming match in front of us all.

"What? Chris is *not* coming to our house. We are *not* prepared for that."

"Well, Sandra, maybe we'll have to change things so he can be under our surveillance. It is obvious things aren't working out now."

As they yelled at each other, the counselor called a break. I quietly slipped out into the adjacent room and listened with a tiny smile, thankful it was no longer me screaming with Ken. The sound of his arguing was too familiar. Ultimately, I would never let Chris stay with Ken because of Ken's abusive behavior toward me. I knew Ken was not about to take Chris into their home, but he put up a good act for the counselors and for Chris.

Chapter 52

I barely made it financially each month and struggled to add extras like clothes for the kids. I bought rice at the gas station because that was the only place I could use a credit card.

This charade had been going on for six years: two years with the divorce, two years with Melo, and now the last two years as an out lesbian. The legal system did not enforce orders given to deadbeat parents. During two court visits, I brought up Ken's negligence and nothing changed. I was tired of behaving reasonably while feeling angry that Ken had not been taking responsibility for his part. The kids were older now and had expensive needs. Sharon, from the ACA group, recommended a lawyer who might work with me financially and get the job done since the system and other lawyers had failed.

The lawyer's office was a long fifty-minute drive up to Lino Lakes. I retained her to try to get child support consistently instead of piecemeal like it had been. After explaining that I had been faithful for six years in cooperating with Ken for his time with the kids, she agreed.

"If we subpoena him, it'll be costly," she warned. Her office was small. She had only a part-time secretary who was not there on Saturdays. Her blond hair was straight and curled slightly under her chin. Her self-confidence encouraged me.

"I know." I gazed out the windows that lined the whole north side of her office. "I am desperate, and you have my word that I will pay you, if it takes forever."

She stared at me for a few seconds, then flipped over some papers and adjusted her pointed, retro-style eyeglasses.

"You have quite a bit of information here, Mary Beth, and it's obvious that he has money with a big sailboat up at Lake Superior and two incomes with his wife. He can afford to get honest and pay child support."

"Do you know that he named his boat *Yahweh's Gift*?" She took her glasses off and shook her head.

Just as I had felt relieved when the kids' counselors took on a bit of my burden of raising them alone, I felt relieved and supported when this lawyer agreed to fight for the money owed me.

We had an agreement that I would pay twenty-five dollars a month until my debt was paid. She cut her prices for me. I made copies of my affidavit for her to lessen my costs. I had to do something.

We subpoenaed Ken to come to my lawyer's office in Lino Lakes with his finances and tax records. Before the meeting, Ken and I were instructed to send each other copies of our checkbook pages for the last year. He got to see where I spent my money, and I saw his. However, he had several pages absent from his checkbook—check numbers 10455–10498 were missing. The old feeling of being under his thumb reemerged.

His wife came with him to the meeting as instructed in the subpoena. She looked mad. On this cool late-summer Saturday, she wore white slacks and a pink V-neck. Ken, in his tan khakis and corduroy sport coat, moved quietly to his chair without his usual banter and puns.

The four of us sat around a tiny table, putting me way too close to Ken. Having my lawyer in charge was comforting, though; I felt I could breathe calmly.

My lawyer started in. "Did you bring your tax returns and your checkbook like I instructed two months ago?"

"Oh." He stood up. "Can I use your phone? I'll have to talk with my tax guy." While he was close by talking, we could hear some of what he said.

"Ha ha! I know, isn't it? Let me know when he gets back."

He squished into his chair next to Sandra. "I can't get ahold of my tax guy."

"You were supposed to have already contacted him and brought copies here today," my lawyer said with a stern voice, hitting him directly with her blue eyes.

He just lifted his hands open and shrugged, with a slight smile.

"Did you bring your salary stubs, Sandra?"

She folded her arms and huffed. "Absolutely not!"

I wrote a note to my lawyer and slid it to her. *Ask about his boat.*

She nodded. "OK, folks, it doesn't look like you're cooperating."

She took a deep breath and picked up another set of papers. Ken and Sandra just stared at us. They were not happy having to answer these financial questions. He had always been in charge of our finances. When we were married, I had to ask him for money whenever I needed it. Then when I earned money at the dance studio, he'd taken it and put it into savings for the kids, which I never saw upon the dissolution of the marriage.

"Ken." She cleared her throat. "Says here in the checkbook that you paid two hundred dollars for a boat slip. Is this monthly?"

He bit the side of his cheek with a finger pushing on the outside. "Not sure."

"Do you own a boat?"

"Yes, a sailboat. It was a gift."

"A gift?" She leaned forward.

"Her name is *Yahweh's Gift.*"

With two incomes for him and his wife, a boat up north, new cars, and a home in their name, it became clear that he had a substantial income. He would have to start paying much more, and consistently. This information nauseated me. His covering up and lying still shocked me. Maybe I was still looking at him as I had when I first met him, as a man of God, a minister to help others find the truth. I couldn't believe that all these years he had found excuses not to pay child support. Honest people of God would bend over backward to make sure they had done even more than their duty and supported their ex-wife and children adequately. I had been accustomed to thinking of Ken as the person who led me to my relationship with Jesus. I'd thought he was honest and a win-win when I said yes to his proposal. His actions were the opposite of what I expected of a man in his position.

When Melo was still with me, one day he had brought over a whole turkey and delivered it with a smile, as if he were the almighty Giver. I needed that turkey. It would have supplied many dinners and sandwiches. But Melo was furious because he hadn't been paying child support. She took the lead. We'd driven to his house with the turkey, and I'd reluctantly left it on his boulevard. We drove off. I'd known she was right, but at that moment, I'd been more focused on the need for food for dinner.

My eyes had opened. There was no miracle cure for my dysfunctional upbringing. No human could protect me and do the right thing. My journey was not glamorous; it was just one step at a time. Finally, I was in charge.

The court decided that Ken's wages would be garnished to pay child support. He'd have to pay $600 a month until Paul turned eighteen. If he had been a genuine, honest man and sought to pay child support from the beginning, it would have been $1,800 a month, or close to it. I let go of the many years of unpaid child support because nothing was in place to retrieve it without a big attorney bill, and I was worn down. I didn't keep track of what he had not paid for the past six years. My friends from Pierre, Ginny and her husband, had been sending me a hundred dollars a month during that time. Not seeking the past amount gave fuel to my simmering anger. But, thankfully, the system had evolved to actively go after the non-custodial parent.

Chapter 53

With a pink slip from Minneapolis Public Schools in hand, I started my summer landscaping job. I'd known this laid-off notice was coming because I was not tenured. I wasn't happy about it, and being laid off every spring was especially hard with kids.

"My job is to beautify Minneapolis," Brad proclaimed. "Have you ever noticed how straight men force a lower voice when they talk?" I blinked to reflect on what my boss had just said and looked up at the hand-painted *trompe l'oeil* sun bursting from the chandelier to make the ceiling look rounded.

Sticking his head in the door, Kevin, who also went by the name *Dottie*, said, "Who's going to Pride this weekend?" He was dressed in a white dress with black polka dots.

"I am." I barely raised my hand to shoulder height.

"We're putting in a brick wall today, Dottie. Do you want to join us?" Todd asked with a smirk.

"No, thank you, Todd, I don't want to ruin my nails." Dottie did an about-face and left.

We hopped into the F-150 after loading shovels and gravel. This was the second summer of my landscaping job for seven dollars an hour. It barely paid the bills between getting laid off and hopefully rehired in the fall.

I wore the same cotton dress to Gay Pride every year, a loose-fitting vintage green plaid, mainly because folks complimented me. I wore it teaching and sometimes as a house dress, which was its original purpose. Even my students liked it. During "Twin Day," one student from Laos said that dress was still common in her home. We posed together in a picture as twins, arms around each other's backs. The green and orange dress was truly vintage, with darts and tiny buttons down the bodice. The seams were so worn that they were coming apart. I also wore white anklets and black Doc Martens that tied at the ankle. The sun bore down on my head as I stood on the curb, smothered by the crowd three rows deep.

My attention turned back to my favorite part of the parade, the "dykes on bikes" who came first. I heard the motors revving in the background before I glimpsed the leather-clad women of all shapes and sizes. They were confident, robust, and tough. The bikes jerked forward and gradually moved, with the women's biker legs stretched out to balance in the slow-moving parade.

I could not wait to see people who were breaking so many of my former rules in their dress, makeup, dancing, nudity, motorcycling, and sex. The feeling of pride overwhelmed me. The men dressed only in barrels tempting the onlookers to peek inside, the marching bands, the women drummers, the men in high heels– it all reversed what I had considered normal. I learned the politics of the marginalized by reading the signs of the parade participants and politicians. I rushed forward to shake hands with Paul Wellstone. Everyone cheered when he and his wife came by. Dottie strutted in her high heels, the same white polka-dotted dress, and a matching wide-brimmed hat that floated as she walked. I longed for the unconventional because it allowed me to forget the restraints that I had let the straight world put on me.

I jumped up with my hand high. "Dottie!" I yelled. She turned and pushed through–no–the crowd parted for her, and she gave me a big hug. Then she sashayed back down the parade route.

Onlookers cried when they saw parents and family members in the P Flagg group marching by with signs that proclaimed "I love my lesbian daughter!" or "My gay son is a loving member of our family." I thought of my mom, who had not spoken to me for a while when I wanted to bring Char to our Easter family dinner. As these family members passed, the crowd quieted and my throat filled with emotion. Heads turned slowly, reading every sign.

My church, St. Joan of Arc, came by holding signs and a big banner: "SJA welcomes you wherever you are in your journey." I waved at members of my LGBTQ+ church group.

Minneapolis Public Schools had a group that included a superinten-dent, a few principals, and brave tenured and nontenured teachers. I want-ed to join them, but I still harbored fears because I was nontenured. I was out in many ways but not completely. With an exhalation, I let them pass and stayed deep in the crowd. I admired those teachers who were out, bold, and free like Melo.

The fire engine brought the parade to a close. Quietly, I stood, not ready or able to wave to Melo, who was jumping on and off the engine with her captain's hat slung back on her head, having a ball. I watched her every move. Bystanders feigned collapsing so the firefighters would come and kiss them till they got up. She waved her cap as her eyes locked on mine.

Chapter 54

After a restless sleep that night with dreams about Melo, I got up early to go to work in my steel-toed boots, rolled-up cutoffs, and a faded "Get in Gear" 10K T-shirt. I felt great in these comfortable clothes that showed off my muscles. Our job was to construct a retaining wall with cement blocks that locked into each other. The blue sky was punctured by a few cumulus clouds. I could smell lilac trees. Using a wheelbarrow, I dumped sand where Todd had shoveled and tamped an even base for the wall. He stressed how important it was to make the surface level. Then, in leather gloves, Brian and I hauled over the bricks, one by one, from the pallet on the boulevard.

"I'm starved!" I leaned on my pointy shovel and wiped my brow. As I was the only woman working for Todd and Brad, they gave me some leeway. Todd was very businesslike but easy to persuade. His short, thick hair was graying even though he was only thirty.

"OK, let's go." We all piled in the big red truck. The truck's back end had two wheels on each side, creating hips with six wheels total.

I made friends with some of the other workers. Brian, a strong, pear-shaped guy, often joked around and made me laugh. His short, prickly hair stood straight up.

Brad and Todd had a bad habit of stopping at fast-food places. The scents of fries and Big Macs filled my nostrils as we walked in the door from the parking lot. A passing car pounded bass beats.

"Do you want to dance?" Brian asked with mocked seriousness as he held his body stiffly, one arm straight up and bent at the wrist.

We danced the minuet, or rather our version of it, with curtsies, bent-over-backward bows, smiles, and twirls, while the deafening booms of the nearby car's music drowned out our laughter.

Every morning, I shouted "Brian!" with my leg back in a racer stance, signaling to Brian I was going to run the short distance of the office and jump into his arms. He'd lift me off my feet. Brad tolerated our shenanigans with a look above his glasses. I felt deeply what it was to be accepted. The past judgments from family and ministry friends softened. I could be myself without the pressure of having to please everyone or live up to their standards. I could be silly if I wanted. That felt very liberating. It seemed ironic to me that the very folks who welcomed me and made me feel normal were the marginalized gay community.

Over the summer months, I dropped in weight and bulged out with muscles. Coming home around five every day, I could hardly move. My whole body hurt. The kids knew I needed at least a half hour with my boots off and feet up. Then I snuck out back behind my fence and stood by the garage to smoke one cigarette that I had bought from a coffee shop on Lyndale. I was trying to quit.

That summer, they promoted me to foreman, putting me in charge of three men. One sluff-off talked about the women he impregnated more than he worked. He had several children already. He was short and overweight.

It was more than empowering for me to look this self-absorbed guy in the eye and say *no* when he'd try to break for lunch early.

After lunch, I climbed into the Bobcat, turned the key, and backed down the two narrow ramps on the trailer.

"OK, heads up! I'm coming through!" I yelled and shifted a lever up to lift a bucket above our heads and out of the way. Then I depressed forward. My breath stalled as I watched the powerful arm lift high. It felt like the Bobcat could fall backward. A few years before, I would not have imagined that I would be driving that vehicle while the men watched.

"Careful of the fences, Mary Beth. Good. Good. Keep going straight," Brad directed. The Bobcat jerked and jumped until I centered it in front of a narrow path only slightly wider than it was. A fence lined each side.

In the cab, the lever slid forward and back effortlessly, as well as the lift knob and bucket control. I noticed that some "men's work" was simple.

Precise and careful, I saved lots of trouble for my bosses with my Bobcat abilities. The roar of the Bobcat carrying boulders in the bucket and slowly dropping them into the back of the F-150 truck was as powerful as the feel of the earth trembling when a boulder dropped on the ground.

The work crew also followed my orders on other jobs for the day. I felt important to have been made a supervisor. "Miguel, we'll have to take out the window well. I'll get a new one at Menards," I said as we stood in the tiny back patio area of a condo complex, surveying the space to be paved.

Miguel laid brick in the basketweave style over a sand base for a client's patio the whole afternoon. "I'll be back in a bit. Make sure the sand is even first. Here." I handed him the bubble level after making sure his bricks were flat. It was satisfying to finish a project and "beautify Minneapolis."

My daughter joined to paint the window casings of a house that the guys and I had roofed the week before. I was glad she had a chance to learn how to use a brush. And deep down, she saw that these gay men were fun and generous. They modeled a bit of my point of view, which she had not completely embraced yet.

"Is this good, Mom?" Gabrielle asked, her face bright with red cheeks. She turned on the short ladder with the brush held high, a glob ready to drop.

"Yes, and use just a little less paint at a time," I instructed.

I had used a nail gun for the first time to roof the same house the previous week. It was on a gradual slope, scary but easy. Some of the workers told stories of nails in their knees from the nail gun. I was careful and slower. I punched in one nail to Brad's four.

Todd and Brad's business did indoor work also. Todd assigned me to put two-by-fours in the basement of a popular local lesbian performer. With my big hair and my tool belt on my hips, I walked in. The singer followed me downstairs to show me the design of the work she wanted.

"So, do you do this work often?" she asked. Her sculpted hair was buzzed all around, the longest being about an inch on top. She pushed her dark-rimmed glasses up the bridge of her nose with her finger.

"Every summer," I said as I pulled the tape measure out of my tool belt and marked sixteen inches on center between studs with a wide flat pencil, then stuck the pencil in my hair.

"Just summers?" She leaned against the side of the stairwell with her shoulder.

"I teach during the school year. It's a good schedule with kids."

She inclined forward. "How many?"

"Three."

Her smile faded at the word *three*, and within seconds, she had disappeared back up to the main floor.

It is interesting how life gets more complicated with kids. I had to work more because I needed a bigger house with more bedrooms. If I did not have children, I may not have pursued such a strenuous physical job. I would not have had to put one foot in front of the other when I was out of energy. The divorce would have been different, much easier and quicker.

The faces of my kids kept me alive when I was at my lowest point. Less than two years had passed since that night I had contemplated ending my life with pills. My children gave me more than my wildest dreams. Despite all the missed weekends and extra jobs, I would not trade them for anything. Together, Gabrielle and I found solutions to whatever issue was at hand. Chris gave me courage as I parented alone. And sensitive Paul missed out on some of my attention because he slipped by unnoticed as the third child while I was putting out fires with the older two. Still, Paul was a ballast whose quiet presence kept me anchored through financial insecurity.

Chapter 55

I turned my attention to buying a home for me and the kids. With the extra teaching job in St. Paul (teaching Spanish in a Catholic grade school), my realtor Bonnie said that I qualified for a loan but would need a $3,000 down payment. I could not count child support as income because it had been irregular for six years. Even with the court order, we could not count on Ken. My mom helped again, even while in the same breath she said, "You can't afford a house." I chose to ignore Mom's comment because I knew her life had been challenging and she was where I had been. It still hurt.

Riding through expensive south Minneapolis searching for a home in Bonnie's cool black Jeep Cherokee, we had toured over a hundred homes in the Washburn school area. I made an offer on a Clinton Avenue house on the east side of 35W. Bumping shoulders with my realtor, I said, "Bonnie, the upstairs is so cool–it's a whole floor just for me. A large blue carpeted bedroom with a private bath." Deep down, I knew I needed a nest for myself and began to give attention to my desires.

"Well, Mary Beth, do you want to make an offer? It's in your price range." I nodded. "Yes!"

We put in the offer. That night I dreamed of how my furniture would look in the house, especially the attic that had been converted into a master bedroom. I fell asleep with a smile.

Bonnie called the next morning. "Mary Beth, someone had a pending offer, and it went through."

The next quiet weekend, I walked from my Second Avenue house to Lake Harriet. I always took different routes just to investigate new neighborhoods. As I walked, I prayed, *Dear Jesus, I've done the research—please help me find the perfect house for me and the kids.*

An open-house sign was planted on Forty-Fourth Street. I looked up at a grand two-story; chestnut-brown cedar siding covered the whole house. It reminded me of my dream home in Barrington. It was surrounded by a tiny yard.

Inside, quite a few people were opening buffet doors, touching the dark-stained oak trim, and oohing. The draw for me was the cozy TV room. Uniform little flowers in tan and maroon lined the papered walls. The drawback was that there was only one bathroom, but the upstairs had four bedrooms. I was thrilled. There was a roughed-out space for a second bathroom, but no running water.

I talked with my realtor, who said, "Let's make an offer, but with the addition of all of us chipping in: you buy the toilet and sink, the owner pays the plumber, and I'll help the plumber by donating my time. What do you think?" Everyone agreed.

I went shopping for a toilet and my very first pedestal sink. I had lusted after the old-fashioned sink most of my home-owning life. The plumber and Bonnie got the water up to my second floor.

Outside of giving birth three times, the single most powerful act I had ever done was to buy my own house.

All my life, I had searched for a place to call home, and this house gave me a chance to finally feel at home in my own body. I felt like a new person, one who could live and survive successfully in this world. The negativity from Ken's comments about how I could not support my family shed off me like scales. Swelling with pride, I saw that by putting one foot in front of the other, I could get jobs and put food on the table.

Relationships had been, and still were, my weakness. Growing up in my family had given me a deficit from the start, but I maneuvered through the murk and found my way. I was drawn to certain controlling personalities and others that imprinted the yang on my yin. But internally, I had grown to love myself and learned to take it easy with my slow process. I still tried to please. My spiritual relationship remained strong. And the relationship I had with my home allowed me to put myself up on a pedestal.

The front living room lacked furniture, but through my two teaching jobs for MPS and St. Paul, I eventually saved enough money to afford furniture. My grandma's early-American buffet with a spoon rack, a round table, chairs, and a lazy Susan was centered in the dining room in front of the built-in buffet.

The kids loved it. Chris's friends lived close by. He sat proudly in the TV room with two girls, one on each side of him, and his friend Jimmy across from them.

The home that I provided was finally making everyone happy. That filled me with joy beyond my wildest dreams. The void I had always felt, that I had tried to fill with a romantic relationship, was quiet. I still wanted that, but it was not paramount.

My home was full of kids and friends with doors constantly opening and closing. Gabrielle finally had an upstairs bedroom–no more basement bugs. Eventually, I replaced her canopy bed with a white wicker headboard, painted two unfinished dressers, and put white porcelain knobs on the drawers. We bought lavender and pink-flowered sheets for her bed and sewed matching curtains for the windows. We used the trim from the top of the sheets as sashes to swing back the curtains. She finally had a princess bedroom. Each of us had our own space.

The boys, especially Paul, were happy to have rooms no one else could enter without their permission. To this day, I look back on the bigness of that move.

My bedroom was huge. Windows on two sides were adorned with my dark-blue paisley Priscilla curtains. My parents' 1950s bedroom furniture clashed with my new bed, but I did not care and was thrilled to have this space. I bought purple-and-green plaid flannel sheets for my cozy heated waterbed.

I had a bedroom for each child, two stories, a front porch, a garage, and a yard with gardening potential. My Sanford staff gave me ideas on gardening. They suggested Jacob's ladder, coral bells, hostas, and columbine—the same flower that my grandpa had in his garden.

Chapter 56

One by one, my neighbors had stopped by to introduce themselves to me during the summer. I invited them over one evening for hors d'oeuvres and drinks. I served a French goat brie and a white Vouvray in the backyard. Outside the fence, I heard a motorcycle drive up.

"Mare, Mare!"

I stood, opened the gate to the fence, and saw Melo on her bike, the motor running, one foot on a pedal and one grounded.

"Come in." I held the gate open; she stood by her motorcycle and turned it off.

"This is Melo," I said to the group of women neighbors. They greeted her.

"How do you know each other?" one asked.

I hesitated for a second while looking at Melo, and she said, "We were together years ago." I beamed, wishing I had said that.

"Oh!" answered a few of them. I could see them trying to understand my life. They seemed comfortable with the information.

After a few minutes, she said her goodbyes.

I was happy to see her come by. I was proud to have had her in my life. She had imprinted upon me honesty and a sense that I could do anything. I had learned to laugh with my kids more, and I danced whenever I could.

In middle school, I played with my students. I noticed that the middle years' students teetered between childhood and adulthood. I did crazy stunts like jumping on a desk and crouching down, scratching my underarms and making monkey sounds, and I did a great elephant cry. For an art project in French, we drew Moroccan architecture. I sang French songs with actions while the students learned the lyrics. I choreographed the *Wizard of Oz* musical the student body presented. The French job at Sanford Junior High increased under my direction from one class to a full-time French teacher. I was able to drop the extra job in St. Paul. Instead of traveling to another city or across town, I had the luxury of teaching in one school and using my prep time to plan. Having credibility as a professional gave me satisfaction. Financially, I could count on a regular salary and child support, which lessened the stress. Todd and Brad came over and replaced the water heater. I paid twenty-five dollars a month until they said I could stop.

It was a huge step to become an independent woman. I paid Mom back for the down payment loan, sending her $300 each month. I no longer tried to prove myself and go over 110 percent.

My new home didn't have living-room furniture for a year. But when the kids and I came home from school, we spent time together. I loved reading detective stories, and the kids would see me sprawled out in a chair reading for hours. My neighbor from across the street gave me gardening advice and plants from her garden. She also frowned when I used a spray bottle of blue chemical fertilizer to help my plants grow.

Paul became more interested in music and continued playing the guitar. Another neighbor knocked on my orchid-painted door at 11:30 p.m. on a sweltering summer night and asked if my son would please stop playing his electric guitar for the whole neighborhood.

Chris continued to live on the edge and try new things. For his senior project, he and a friend accidentally dug up my peonies and planted a garden. He brought home an A, along with actual pots, from his pottery class. One piece of pottery was in the shape of a face with its tongue sticking out.

Gabrielle got to live in her new room on the second floor for a year before she went to college. We had to put our heads together to figure out how to pay for it. She worked, and Ken and I paid what we could.

Ten years before, all my hopes had been based on the abilities of a man. He approved everything. I did not have agency to secure my aspirations. My only vision was to find a man to fulfill my dreams.

I have come out as Mary Beth Spray, a name I've always had, and now it bears substance; it has meat.

I have leaned on men, priests, leaders, and husband, thinking I was more if I clung to someone else. During the second half of my life, I looked to women to enhance my identity.

Now I choose every part of my future, and I make the decisions. I am no longer invisible. I work through my shame when it surfaces. I believe in my abilities and carry out my goals one step at a time.

The alchemy of energy inside me had catapulted my family into our future. Now I inhaled slowly and gently. The court baggage was gone; Ken wasn't a threat anymore because I had come out, and the support check came regularly. My children noticed my shift also. My prayer life with God, my higher power, gave me peace—the one relationship that would never leave me.

My new mantra has lasted to this day. "I don't have to be perfect, nor do I have to please anyone!"

The oxygen around our house was breathable. Written on my kids' faces was a sense that I was in charge and would take care of them. Gabrielle's intensity was intact, and she smiled more. Chris looked all of us in the eyes. Paul occupied himself for hours with friends, guitar, and Michael Crichton novels. Our physical dwelling felt immense; all the unspoken and the abysmal messes had cleared out for the time being.

"Intoxications of life's morning! Enchanted years!
The wing of a dragonfly trembles!
Oh, reader, whoever you may be, do you have such memories?"

—Victor Hugo

Acknowledgments

I want to thank my sister Linda, who has been unwavering in support through my adult years. My sister-in-law, Debbie, who is positive and steadfast in support and love. My Patio group of teaching friends: Ellen, Melissa, Cynthia, and Sarah, who have met with me once a month for twenty-five years. Our gathering included laughter, crying, books, and sharing our lives, meals, and wine. I would like to thank Abbie P as proofreader and project manager. She erased any doubt and answered all questions. There are several Marys. Mary P, for untangling my SFD; Mary CM, for editing support and teaching classes; and Mary Lou, for being my friend. Kate read two drafts and said, "Do it!" before I had confidence. Katy P and Shari A, for their thoughtful and comprehensive beta reads.